Big Little Things

Big Little Things
50 Tools for Building a Better Classroom

2nd Edition

Ron Nash

ROWMAN & LITTLEFIELD
Lanham • Boulder • New York • London

Published by Rowman & Littlefield
An imprint of The Rowman & Littlefield Publishing Group, Inc.
4501 Forbes Boulevard, Suite 200, Lanham, Maryland 20706
www.rowman.com

86-90 Paul Street, London EC2A 4NE

Copyright © 2024 by Ron Nash

All rights reserved. No part of this book may be reproduced in any form or by any electronic or mechanical means, including information storage and retrieval systems, without written permission from the publisher, except by a reviewer who may quote passages in a review.

British Library Cataloguing in Publication Information Available

Library of Congress Cataloging-in-Publication Data

Names: Nash, Ron, author.
Title: Big little things : 50 tools for building a better classroom / Ron Nash.
Description: 2nd edition. | Lanham, Maryland : Rowman & Littlefield, 2024. | Includes bibliographical references and index.
Identifiers: LCCN 2024022224 (print) | LCCN 2024022225 (ebook) | ISBN 9781475874655 (cloth) | ISBN 9781475874662 (paperback) | ISBN 9781475874679 (ebook)
Subjects: LCSH: Classroom management.
Classification: LCC LB3013 .N273 2024 (print) | LCC LB3013 (ebook) | DDC 371.102/4—dc23/eng/20240521
LC record available at https://lccn.loc.gov/2024022224
LC ebook record available at https://lccn.loc.gov/2024022225

CONTENTS

Acknowledgments xv

Introduction 1

CHAPTER 1 Easy Doesn't Do It................................... 7
Anyone who wants to get better at getting better has to move outside his or her comfort zone, and teachers need to take this into account when planning lessons for the classroom.

CHAPTER 2 Providing Choice..................................... 11
This generation of students has complete control over the phones they use for several hours per day. Having plenty of choice is something to which they have become accustomed, and teachers can build choice into their instructional planning and, as we'll see in this chapter, into their furniture configuration.

CHAPTER 3 "But I Told Them!" 15
Simply explaining procedures or *posting* a set of laminated procedures for the classroom is never enough. If location, location, location is the key to success in real estate, then modeling, followed by practice, practice, practice is its equivalent in the classroom. To be effective, classroom procedures need to become routine.

CHAPTER 4 Congruence 19
If a teacher's list of commandments for the classroom include *Thou shalt be on time for class!*, the teacher who walks into class late every day is guilty of incongruent behavior. Walking the talk is important for teachers who expect the class rules to be followed.

CONTENTS

CHAPTER 5   The Fear Factor.................................... 23
We want students to contribute as individuals or as members of collaborative groups, but if they don't feel safe doing that, then engagement—and learning—will suffer. Teachers should work to eradicate fear from the classroom.

CHAPTER 6   Reassuring Redundancies........................... 27
Teachers who plan elaborate lesson plans with technology as a key component need to make sure they have built-in redundancies that will answer the musical question, "What happens when Plan A doesn't work?" (Answer: Plan B)

CHAPTER 7   Everyone in the (Learning) Pool 31
Traditional adult-centered classrooms are often structured so that the only one in the learning pool is the teacher. I learned more about U.S. history in my first semester of teaching than I did in college, and that was because I did most of the reading and talking. In truly interactive classrooms, everyone, teachers and students alike, is engaged in the learning process; the teacher is simply the learner-in-chief.

CHAPTER 8   The Lighter Side 35
Some of my teachers were naturally funny. Others had to work at it, not always successfully. But humor has a place in the classroom. Laughter lightens moods and helps release neurotransmitters in the brain. We'll look at appropriate forms of humor in this chapter.

CHAPTER 9   "You in the Yellow Shirt!"........................... 39
Names are important to the people who own them, and when teachers take the time to learn and pronounce the names of students early in the school year, it is appreciated. Pointing to someone whose hand is in the air isn't.

CHAPTER 10   Trigger the Calm.................................... 43
Fred Jones (2007) reminds us that calm is strength, and upset is weakness. Don't put that last nerve in sight for the student who is more than happy to step on it.

CHAPTER 11   Model and Teach Effective Listening Skills............. 47
Before students can work together successfully in groups, they need to learn and practice listening skills essential for collaborative learning. This begins with the modeling of those skills by teachers.

CONTENTS

CHAPTER 12 The Best is (Often) Silence........................ 51
Purposeful silence can be an effective teaching tool. A silent pause following a period of lecture serves to focus the minds of students not used to the absence of teacher talk. The mighty pause can also be used effectively after a question is asked or after an answer has been given.

CHAPTER 13 Press and Release................................. 55
Lectures can often seem to go on forever in the minds of students. Teachers who "press" students with lectures or a period of direct instruction need to provide a "release" mechanism of some sort. Allowing students to reflect on new information independently or with a partner can provide that welcome—and necessary—release.

CHAPTER 14 Kids Gotta Move.................................. 59
Among the things I learned as a kid is this: Kids need to move. And among the things John Medina (2014) has learned from a lifetime of studying the brain is that exercise improves cognition. The simple act of standing increases blood flow to the brain, carrying with it oxygen and glucose for energy. Great teachers find ways to include movement and exercise in their lessons.

CHAPTER 15 Perma Pairs.. 63
There comes a time when teachers want students to share some new information; the sooner students share, the more they will retain and understand. If each student in the class has a permanent partner, the pairing can be done quickly, and with someone whom the students have come to know well.

CHAPTER 16 Choosing Partners................................. 67
A friend of mine used to have his biology students up, pairing, and sharing on the first day of classes. Also, they changed partners frequently. His goal was to let them know they would be meeting and interacting with everyone in the room, not just with their close friends. There are many effective ways to provide—or allow students to choose—paired partners.

CHAPTER 17 Priming... 71
Many students are perfectly comfortable speaking to a room full of classmates; others are more reticent to share publicly at first. For the teacher who wants to surface opinions or questions, let students do so in pairs, rather than in a whole-class setting, until they feel comfortable with developed social skills. Larger conversations can develop naturally from smaller ones as the confidence of students builds.

CONTENTS

CHAPTER 18 Whole-Class Discussions............................ 75
Teachers have an important role in facilitating whole-class discussions, and such discussions are dependent upon the listening skills introduced in chapter 11.

CHAPTER 19 Have at It! 79
I have had lots of opportunities to take part in the planning of this program or that project at the building and district level, and I often think we plan things into extinction. *We scare people with the plan*, when we could simply get out of the starting blocks on a small scale, seek feedback, and adjust as necessary.

CHAPTER 20 Process-Related Dipstick Checks 83
Dipstick checks can tell a car owner if the car needs oil. Frequent feedback can tell teachers and students where to go or what to do next. Classroom processes can be improved if teachers take the time and find a way to get feedback—then make necessary adjustments.

CHAPTER 21 Reflective Learners.................................. 87
Teachers, and I was guilty of this, often rush from one summative assessment to the next, spewing out new information in great dollops, while giving students little time to process anything. By so doing, we risk turning them into notetakers and pretend listeners, and we do not allow them to *be* students. Teachers can—and should—allow time for students to reflect, self-assess, seek feedback, and otherwise come to grips with their own errors as part of the continuous improvement process.

CHAPTER 22 Purposeful and Thoughtful Praise 91
Scattering praise like confetti generally does little good in a classroom. If everybody is doing a "Good Job!" today, then the whole idea of a good job is meaningless—and the praise itself carries no weight. If "Excellent work!" follows some specific, timely, and useful feedback, it serves to put an exclamation point on the feedback itself.

CHAPTER 23 The Smooth Shifting of Transitional Gears............ 95
Teachers shift gears between activities or assignments several times a day. Those transitions can be smooth or rough, and it is the teacher who makes the difference. Hundreds of smooth transitions over the course of a year save time, prevent confusion, and improve the credibility of the teacher in the eyes of her students.

CONTENTS

CHAPTER 24 Avoid Unnecessary Decisions 99
The teacher who gives a half-dozen verbal instructions, then turns students loose on the assignment, forces them to make decisions without adequate information. A written, perhaps posted, set of instructions keeps students from guessing (often incorrectly) and experiencing confusion.

CHAPTER 25 Transfer Skills to the Collaborative Setting 103
Pausing for reflection and emphasis, using correctly pronounced names in pairs or group settings, and brainstorming are all skills that can be put to good use when teachers—or students, increasingly—are in presentation mode. These skills can all be practiced during the first days and weeks of school, then transferred to project-based learning tasks later on in the year.

CHAPTER 26 Provide Easy Access to Complex Tasks.............. 107
When 30 sixth graders are not sure where to go to get the materials they will need for a task, confusion follows, and teachers spend time on the clean-up in aisles 3, 4, and 6. In this chapter, we'll look at some organizational tips that will make things run more smoothly in classrooms.

CHAPTER 27 The First Few Minutes 111
Students in the hallway approaching a classroom are generally in one of two mind frames: (1) This class is always different and enjoyable, or (2) *If I see one more worksheet . . . !* The first few minutes of any class will set the tone, and this begins at the doorway. Make those first few minutes memorable.

CHAPTER 28 Last Impressions 115
My lessons often ended with the bell, and with me shouting at the backs of departing students, "Don't forget your homework!" or "Hunker down for that test Tuesday!" The best teachers I know shift gears during those last minutes of a class period or block, and that often includes an upbeat song guaranteed to send students out of the room in a good mood and with a light step.

CHAPTER 29 That's the Plan.................................... 119
The number and quality of student presentations is increasing each year as more and more teachers, schools, and districts commit to collaborative student work and project-based learning. Teachers can model the effective use of PowerPoint (or other such programs), graphics, charts, voice, and many other presentation norms. This and the next few chapters will concentrate on presentations.

CONTENTS

CHAPTER 30 If the Font Fits, Share It 125
More times than I care to remember, a presenter, or teacher-as-presenter, will display text on the screen that is too small for anyone, even those up front, to read. Then the presenter says something to this effect: "I'm sorry if you can't read this." If they can't read it, don't put it up there. In this chapter, we'll provide a few suggestions when it comes to fonts and graphics.

CHAPTER 31 Visuals Always Win (Make that Work for You!)....... 129
Visuals are powerful, so powerful that they can compete with you, rather than help you. We'll look at some things to avoid when using visuals in presentation mode.

CHAPTER 32 Attention to Voice 133
A presenter's voice is a tool, and there are ways to use that tool effectively in classrooms and in student presentations. Teachers can model the effective use of voice, then teach the skills to students.

CHAPTER 33 Arms Control 137
Gestures can serve as a great tool in the hands of a good presenter. But gestures can also serve to derail a presentation, as I found out when I watched myself on videotape many years ago. I was afflicted with "flailing arms syndrome" in classrooms and in more formal presentations to adults. Gestures are worthy of consideration for teachers and students alike.

CHAPTER 34 Hitting the Right Notes 141
Music is a big part of my presentations to adults, and I know many teachers who use it successfully in classrooms at every grade level. Music is a great mood lifter, and it has many specific uses in classrooms.

CHAPTER 35 As You Were...................................... 145
When teachers work the room while students are in groups, they want to see what students are doing and ask a few guiding questions. What the teacher should *not* want is to have everything come to a full stop when she approaches a group. Students can be taught to concentrate on the business at hand when the teacher approaches.

CHAPTER 36 Bringing Them Back 149
When thirty students are standing as they participate in fifteen conversations, a teacher needs a single way to bring them back to her—every time. We'll explore ways to accomplish that in this chapter.

CHAPTER 37 One-at-a-Time Directions 153

An incomplete or confusing set of directions can derail the best tasks or projects. The goal with one-at-a-time directions for activities is to avoid confusion on the part of students right up front, so that everything proceeds smoothly. I have seen what can happen when students have no idea where to start or what to do. Teacher credibility can suffer when students are frustrated with procedures or directions. The answer is as simple as it is straightforward.

CHAPTER 38 Avoid Competing with the Lawnmower 157

When boredom sets in, the minds of students tend to wander, and quite normal sounds like the HVAC system or the lawnmower outside the classroom window holds Eddie's attention in a way that the lesson has failed to do. The best teachers I have observed over the years get their students off the bench and into the game in meaningful and productive ways, engaging them so that distractions are few.

CHAPTER 39 Teach Students to Paraphrase for Understanding 161

People like to know that when they are talking, the person with whom they are engaged in conversation is listening. Body language will do that, and so will a short silence after the speaker is done talking, followed by a bit of paraphrasing on the part of the listener. The paraphrase signals to the speaker that the listener is truly listening, and they want to understand.

CHAPTER 40 The Two-Minute Drill 165

One sure way to build rapport with students, something that accelerates the creation of a learning community, is to hold frequent and short conversations with students every day, whether it is between classes or after school. Our walkers had to wait for the buses to leave, and that few minutes was the perfect time for conversations between them and the teachers on my seventh-grade team.

CHAPTER 41 Connecting with Stories 169

My favorite college professor had a gold watch on a chain, one that he kept in the vest of his three-piece suit. When he pulled out the watch and placed it on the table, winding the chain around the watch, we knew a story was coming—something that made us sit forward over our desks in anticipation. We'll look at the power of storytelling in this chapter.

CONTENTS

CHAPTER 42 Getting Better at Getting Better.................... 173
Feedback is useful only when it is provided while a group project or individual assignment is in process. There are many actions teachers can take, including the posing of guiding questions, to help students improve their performance in virtually all areas. The notation, "Could do better!" after the final grade is not helpful—or particularly motivational—to Eddie. Learning shouldn't be competitive; it's about getting better, and it's about getting better at doing that.

CHAPTER 43 Tolerate Ambiguity and Encourage Questions 177
It is perfectly okay to not be in possession of the answers or to change one's mind when new information comes to light. It ought to be acceptable to be wrong while one is engaged in the learning process. It should be fine to furrow the brow and admit one hasn't a clue. And every classroom environment should be deemed safe enough by students for questions that will help bring our thoughts into focus.

CHAPTER 44 Harness the Power of Novelty 183
There was a sameness to my first years as a teacher, and my students could easily predict, once they spied the overhead projector front and center, how similar Tuesday would be to Monday. Students appreciate a teacher who breaks the same-old-same-old mold by introducing novel experiences into the daily lesson plan. Information presented in a novel way helps students focus and commit to memory.

CHAPTER 45 Physical and Mental State Changes.................. 187
Students who sit and listen—or pretend to listen—to a teacher talk have learned how to play the game: sit up straight, smile, nod occasionally, and avoid watching the wall clock. As a new teacher, I thought that nod was proof that I was on the right track with my informative and apparently captivating lecture. Perhaps not.

CHAPTER 46 Avoid the Blame Game........................... 191
As a new teacher, I succumbed to playing the blame game in the faculty lounge. My colleagues and I blamed low test scores and a lack of student energy on textbooks, administrators, parents, and on everything and everyone except us. This accomplishes nothing, solves nothing, and helps no one.

CONTENTS

CHAPTER 47 Those Too Busy to Complain........................ 195
The best teachers I have met over the years are simply too busy to
spend time complaining about things outside their control. They work at
mastering the skills necessary to succeed. They use time wisely, and they
avoid the negaholics in the building.

CHAPTER 48 The Extra Mile................................... 199
I have known teachers who made it a point to be at the back door when
the bell rings at the end of the day, in a hurry to get to the parking lot.
Then there are teachers who go the extra mile for the kids during and
after the contractual school hours. They are at school sporting events and
concerts, something students appreciate.

CHAPTER 49 The Power of Collaboration........................ 203
Teachers tend to shy away from collaboration with colleagues for the very
simple reason that there is risk involved in opening up their processes and
their plans to others. Yet some of the best reflection is social, and as long
as teachers believe such reflection is formative, rather than evaluative, they
may be willing to share, plan, and work together with colleagues in order
to get better at getting better.

CHAPTER 50 Looking Back at Those Who Look Forward.......... 207
Traveling and presenting has allowed me to meet some incredible
educators, all of whom talk about students, not about themselves or how
many years they have before retirement. I'll close by looking at what
those incredible student advocates have in common.

Afterword 211

References 215

Index 223

ACKNOWLEDGMENTS

Many thanks to Carrie Brandon, Crystal Branson, Jasmine Holman, and April Snider at Rowman & Littlefield for their support during all stages of the acquisition and production process of this book. Arun Rajakumar and his copy editing team at Deanta did a great job of catching my mistakes and making suggestions to improve the manuscript.

Also, I always appreciate the willingness of teachers and administrators to contribute to one of my books. Thanks to Dean Armstrong, Brittan Bell, Darcy Cupp, Kathy Galford, Emily Konrad, Mary Marshall, Gene Soltner, and Joy White for their contributions to *Big Little Things*.

A very special thanks to Dr. Rich Allen for allowing me to use the cartoons in this book. Without Rich Allen, I would not have taken the huge risk of starting my own educational consulting business eighteen years ago. I owe him a great debt of gratitude for his continued friendship and support.

Those years have added up to eighteen books and one wonderful journey, one which has taken me to more than twenty states to present and into hundreds of classrooms to observe and coach several hundred teachers. As always, I thank my wife Candy for encouraging me these many years.

INTRODUCTION

My work as a presenter, author, and teacher coach has taken me into hundreds of classrooms in more than twenty states in the past seventeen years, and I have met with and observed teachers whom I have found to be incredibly competent, confident, effective, and eminently worthy of their students' trust and respect. Those great teachers have at least two things in common:

1. They are willing to invest time and effort into building relationships, not just between themselves and their students, but between and among the students themselves. The body language of the students in those classrooms tells me *they want to be there every day*. Those exceptional teachers have worked ceaselessly to build highly successful and dynamic communities of learners, with themselves as learners-in-chief.

2. Those great teachers are willing to take risks on behalf of students. Some take those risks right out of the gate as new teachers, while others realize after a few years that what they are doing is not working—for them *or* their students—and they commit to substantive changes in their classroom environment and in their instructional methodology. Those decisions may not come easy, but every teacher I have met and observed who has made the leap from a teacher-centered classroom to one that is more student-centered has never looked back.

Building and district administrators must give teachers time and space to make decisions that will no doubt shift teachers—and students—out

INTRODUCTION

of their comfort zones. "In order for learning to emerge," writes France (2023), "learners and teachers alike must have agency to make decisions in the moment." Further,

> They must feel emboldened by the process of learning to grapple with its uncertainty and continue growing. And, finally, they must know it is safe to take risks, make mistakes, and otherwise respond to the learning conversations that are happening all around them. (p. 118)

And in the classrooms of great teachers, no matter the subject area or grade level, paired and group conversations abound. In a Pre-K classroom many years ago, I watched as three students used plastic microphones to "interview" partners. The teacher told me it was the first step in building student-to-student relationships. I still retain a mental image of that classroom and those kids.

I have found, and this was true in my own years in the classroom, that veteran teachers who have taught in the same building for many years—and maybe the same classroom—get comfortable with a routine that seems to have worked for them. What works for teachers may not work for students, however. When I observe the body language of students during classroom observations, I often conclude that they are not engaged in any substantive way with the lesson. Many—perhaps most—have checked out mentally. If purposeful engagement and continuous improvement is the goal, everyone's "relative comfort" may not be conducive to meeting it. We learn best *outside* our comfort zones, where we are truly challenged.

Teachers are heavily influenced by their own experiences as students, and I was no exception. I grew up—and began my teaching career—in the latter years of the Industrial Age. I worked one summer in a machine shop, punching holes in pieces of steel. I and my fellow employees were creatures of the clock, the hands of which seemed to move at a snail's pace. The bell rang and we took a short break. The bell rang and I snatched my lunch pail from a shelf. That same bell, thankfully, sent me home at the end of the day. Bells were a staple, too, in high school. Most high school classes were decidedly teacher-centered, and we shifted into passive mode once we were in our seats. Most of my teachers back in the day seemed to agree that the information students ought to absorb was best delivered orally. And, for the most part, my college classes didn't disabuse me of that notion.

INTRODUCTION

I neither heard nor saw much during the pursuit of my education degree that caused me to make any substantive pedagogical changes in my own first classroom in 1972. I cleaned and polished the glass top on the overhead projector, stocked up on extra bulbs and a few black markers, and proceeded to give my eighth graders the benefit of my vast knowledge. Had anyone suggested I should get students up, moving, and sharing information, I would have recoiled in horror. Those student desks were there for a reason! My idea of an instructional innovation was colored chalk.

When teachers move beyond compliance-and-control environments into highly interactive settings, where students develop considerable social capital as they converse with classmates on a regular basis, the interactions become more complex, thus introducing Murphy's Law into the instructional equation. A second-grade teacher whose students did such a commendable job with paraphrasing told me it took weeks of practice—with all the accompanying missteps and unforced errors—to get to where they were on that October day. But she never looked back, and she kept improving what *she* did so her students could improve what *they* did.

There are seemingly little things that can throw a monkey wrench into the proceedings and bring the best-laid plans to a grinding halt, to the consternation of a teacher who thought she had everything covered, figured out, planned for, and otherwise under control. There isn't a teacher alive, I would guess, who has not reached the halfway point in a lesson, only to discover the train took a detour or simply left the tracks. A few examples:

- **Example 1:** Every teacher gives directions for activities. Directions are necessary, of course, and teachers completely familiar with a well-worn set of directions may choose to give five or six *verbal* directions at one time. I watched as a sixth-grade teacher did just that, then spent the next quarter of an hour dealing with "popcorn hands" from students who could not handle that many directions at once. Giving directions one at a time (chapter 37 in this book) would have allowed for a smooth transition into an otherwise excellent lesson. Knowing that tool was available to her would have saved that teacher and her students' considerable frustration and confusion.

INTRODUCTION

- **Example 2:** I sat near the back of a hotel ballroom as a presenter displayed a few paragraphs on the screen in the front of the room. The presenter was facing the workshop participants and did not realize that the point size of the paragraphs was too small for anyone to read, at least beyond the first few rows. Had the presenter run through the PowerPoint before the session—and moved around the room while progressing through the slides—she would have been able to catch the mistake and fix it. In classrooms and ballrooms, preparation is no little thing.

- **Example 3:** One teacher told her students to find partners and stand somewhere in the room to await her instructions. The furniture in the classroom was not set up in a way that facilitated standing pairs—or movement. The students meandered among the desks, looking for close friends and taking far too long to find someone with whom to stand. There were also a few trios and quartets in the room because students could not decide with whom they would pair. The teacher finally called the room to order and tried to sort it all out, which turned out to be no little—or enjoyable—thing.

These three examples of plans gone awry had simple fixes that would have prevented the frustration, confusion, and overall angst on the part of everyone involved. A seemingly *little* thing, like getting students in standing pairs, can become a *big* headache for teachers. An ounce of prevention in the planning may well be worth a pound of cure when a well-intentioned lesson goes off the tracks. This new and expanded second edition of *Big Little Things* provides a total of fifty chapters filled with practical tools for avoiding the kinds of problems in the examples above.

This book, along with the others I have written over the past seventeen years, emphasizes the importance of helping students build the kinds of social skills they will need to succeed not only in the global economy, but also in life. Collaborative teams in the workplace are becoming more common, and the teams may be comprised of team members from all corners of the globe. Also, writes Tony Wagner (2014), "The ability to express one's views clearly in a democracy and to communicate effectively across cultures is an important citizenship as well" (p. 34).

INTRODUCTION

Communication skills, including those related to writing, speaking, and listening, should be taught in our schools. This means teacher-centered classrooms, where lecture is dominant, must give way to those that are more student-centered and highly interactive.

The best teachers I have observed over three decades model excellent listening skills, work to reduce fear in the classroom environment, establish routines that make things run smoothly every day, allow adequate time for reflection, harness the power of visuals, provide plenty of choice for a generation that demands it, and insist on lots of challenge and collaborative opportunities for their students. This expanded second edition of *Big Little Things* will help new and veteran teachers accomplish these goals in ever-more collaborative classroom environments.

The kinds of tools that allow teachers to succeed are not expensive. Good teaching isn't about the amount of money spent; it is about the time and effort invested in attending to the little things that create the kind of learning environment where students—*and teachers*—want to be every day. Change always involves a certain amount of risk, and great teachers are not afraid to take risks on behalf of the children they serve. Along our journey, we'll hear from many of those teachers who use these practical strategies successfully every day.

My hope is that this second edition will serve as a springboard for further research, thoughtful individual reflection, and much discussion among educators concerning the important topics covered in these fifty chapters.

Read on.

CHAPTER 1
EASY DOESN'T DO IT

I once made the mistake of telling my fitness center trainer, in response to her query as to how I was doing in the middle of a workout, that I felt pretty good. Wrong answer. "Then I'm not working you hard enough," came the reply, and she proceeded to increase the intensity of the training session. Apparently, as it turns out, I'm not the sharpest tack in the drawer because I kept giving the same response to the same question. And she upped the ante each time.

In fact, I have always been appreciative of fitness trainers who pushed me, because I understand that I can't make progress without moving outside my comfort zone. In the free-weight room, my current trainer moves me ever upward as far as weights go, because he understands that progress lies in that *dis*comfort zone. Easy, it turns out, doesn't do it when it comes to continuous improvement in the fitness center.

The same is true with the learning process in classrooms. Posey (2019), referring to Vygotsky's concept of the Zone of Proximal Development (ZPD), writes that "a learner's optimal level can improve with guidance, scaffolds, and encouragement from a skilled educator or peer or by using resources in the environment" (p. 68). In order to grow when it comes to skills of any kind, the challenge—and the forward progress—come outside our comfort zone. Students who "do their own work" while seated and quiet day after day are not likely to grow or move outside what has become a pretty passive and unchallenging reality. A commitment to collaboration on the part of a teacher changes that reality. In a true collaborative classroom environment, help and feedback for students can come from a variety of sources, including peers willing and able to do a bit of coaching for classmates who may be floundering in the presence of

CHAPTER 1

some new learning or, for them, a difficult task. Students learn to help and depend on each other for the smooth and efficient running of the group and the completion of sometimes complex tasks or projects.

There is a temptation on the part of teachers seeking a smooth path forward for themselves to "go easy" on kids with worksheets and videos, along with an overabundance of teacher talk. Students who are required to listen (or pretend to listen) and take notes are really not being challenged at all. And this limits growth in terms of learning. "In short," write Fogarty, Kerns, and Pete (2018), "if we are not pushed or stretched, we do not grow." However, "If we are pushed too much, we become overly frustrated. But if we are pushed at an ideal level—just beyond our reach—we grow optimally" (p. 75).

It does not take long in a classroom for an observer to conclude one of three things:

1. Students are being pushed to the point of frustration, without adequate scaffolding and multiple feedback mechanisms at the ready. They may also be in a state of open rebellion, something I have observed on a good many occasions in classrooms.

2. Teachers are not pushing students at all, but keeping them well within their comfort zones with busy work. The body language from students says many of them are resentful as they come to the realization that the "work" they are doing in the classroom is not helping them move forward. It is busy work of little or no value.

3. There is little frustration evident on the part of students who are operating smoothly and successfully in an interactive and collaborative environment, rich in feedback from teachers and classmates. Students operate with clear learning targets, the reaching of which will take them into the zone of proximal development and toward considerable accomplishments and worthwhile goals.

I have had the good fortune to coach and observe in classrooms where continuous improvement is a given, and where the adult in the room realizes she is not the only teacher inside those four walls. "Daily reaching and struggling to grow skills and abilities can be enjoyable, but only if one receives continual feedback noting this growth" (Fogarty, Kerns, and Pete, 2018, p. 78). In classrooms where students are working individually or in collaborative efforts, classmates who are further along in their growth can be invaluable assets for those who are not. In my first classrooms as a teacher, I regularly exhausted myself while providing feedback constantly while students worked; at least all that exercise kept me thin. In superhero terms, I was "Checklist and Rubric Man" every day. I wanted students to "do their own work," with me as the CFO (Chief Feedback Officer).

As students work toward clear learning targets when it comes to projects and other collaborative tasks, they can self-assess in their groups, asking questions like, "Where are we in relation to the learning target?" or "What is our next step?" or "What does the new information we just received tell us?" I was the one asking the questions as my students worked: "Are you done with that worksheet yet?" or "Does anyone have questions? If so, raise your hand and I'll get to you before the end of the class period, hopefully. Be patient." There is no reason for students who have available to them multiple sources of immediate feedback to have to exercise more than a modicum of patience. The feedback and the answers can be close at hand.

As with progress in fitness training, easy doesn't do it in classrooms. When I said, "Don't worry, this is easy," as I wandered around the room while students answered questions at the end of a section in their history text, I did them no favors. No one was being challenged. Those who knew just where to look in section 4 of chapter 5 of the textbook for the answers to the low-level questions on offer, were bored out of their minds. Others waited until I sidled up beside their desks, knowing I would probably steer them in the right direction. Others could not have cared less. There was little about those stock questions that was of use to my students, other than providing something to glance at briefly before a test or quiz.

Build a Better Classroom by Moving Students Outside Their Comfort Zones

In collaborative environments, students who have spent years in passive classroom settings find themselves with more responsibility. Their

CHAPTER 1

involvement in paired discussions and group projects forces students to develop communication skills they may not have had to use before. They must learn to listen and to coach a bit when a teammate gets stuck or is confused about something related to the task or project on which they are working. Oral language skills suddenly become indispensable, and this pushes them outside their comfort zones and into a world where they are, along with their teammates, responsible for meeting learning targets and growing intellectually. All this may be new to them, and it will no doubt prove difficult, but given the right tools and the right amount of gentle but relentless pressure, they can learn to work, grow, and succeed in a collaborative and highly interactive classroom environment.

Here are some questions that may help you and your students as you move them out of their comfort zones and into a more collaborative framework:

- Is what you are doing every day pushing students hard enough? Too hard? If the answer to the first question is no, and if the answer to the second question is yes, what changes will you make?

- What skills will they need so that they can function effectively in groups? What is the best way to teach those skills?

- How many sources of feedback can you identify and bring into play for students who are working on projects or tasks in the classroom? Could you find time to discuss the whole idea of feedback and its importance to the continuous improvement process with students? How can they provide feedback without judging peers?

- How can you ensure that members of one group can and will coach members of another when invited to do so?

CHAPTER 2
PROVIDING CHOICE

Many things distinguish iGen'ers from previous generations, including the fact that they have never known anything other than cell phones. Those who claim membership in Generation X can remember rotary phones, and my Boomer mates and I can, perhaps, recall two tin cans and a string. Something else that separates the current generation from those preceding it is that iGen'ers require lots of choice (Twenge, 2017). They have total control of their cell phones, and they have seemingly limitless choices as to what they see and with whom they want to communicate via text or through any number of social media sites. Their attention span is driven by the next beep telling them someone else is in the game or on the phone. It is therefore frustrating when they enter a classroom where choice is limited or nonexistent.

Kids who are used to changing channels and holding forth with several friends at once on that hand-held device come into classrooms where a compliance-and-control climate is still in vogue—*and it is entirely foreign to them.* Compliance and control might have been well suited to an industrial age when showing up

Figure 2.1 Brittan Bell's Third-Grade Classroom Is a Model of Flexible Seating. Students May Choose Where They Want to Sit Each Day. *Source:* Photo by Brittan Bell.

CHAPTER 2

on time and following directions was all that was needed in the workplace. Bells in schools prepared students for the bells that rang in the factories. I had that summer job in a machine shop, and it did not require much by way of divergent thinking on my part. I did the same thing day after day, which was pretty much what I did in school.

And classrooms that were set up on the factory model, with thirty identical pieces of student furniture, are still in place in many districts around the country. This is so because it has always been so, but today's students appreciate it when they walk into a classroom where choice is available when it comes to the seating arrangements. Brittan Bell, a third-grade teacher at Lovejoy Elementary School in Des Moines, Iowa, was able, with the support of her principal, to get rid of the standard classroom furniture in their classrooms, replacing it (figure 2.1) with exercise balls, wobble stools, floor pillows, web chairs, and surfboard seats. For those who prefer to stand, there is a standing table (with available stools as an option). Regimentation is out in Bell's classroom, and choice is in.

Bell can speak to the reality that when more choice is given, the number of office referrals goes down markedly. She told me her students loved having this choice of seating: "I have seen students pick new spots near new people each day. I would attribute the hugely positive classroom environment I have established to the fact that students are continually sitting by new people each and every day." One consequence of all this is that office referrals have dropped to almost zero since the implementation of the program. Bell reports that "this type of seating has HUGELY improved the collaborative environment" (personal communication, March 29, 2019).

Choice can also be provided when it comes to setting up classroom norms at the beginning of the year. As reported by Boss and Larmer (2018), math teacher Telannia Norfar "proposes a mini-project that poses this driving question: *How can we create a fair and engaging learning environment for math?*" (p. 20). Brainstorming in all Norfar's classes, followed by votes that help students reach a consensus, results not only in a set of student norms (possess a growth mindset, call classmates by their names, be responsible for your work, be a good team player, and more), but in a corresponding set of teacher norms as well: (teach in different ways, call students by their names, care about students' feelings, help students understand, be respectful, have a growth mindset, and more) (p.

21). Allowing students to have a say in the classroom expectations gives them a voice and helps them become responsible members of Norfar's classroom community.

I visited a North Carolina elementary school with the highest reading scores in the state for many years running. For thirty minutes every day, everyone in the building (including the adults) was expected to read silently. Everything else came to a halt while students and adults located whatever book they had chosen to read that day, and they spent a half hour reading for enjoyment. Needless to say, that school had among the highest reading scores in the state year after year.

As a young and admittedly wet-behind-the-ears teacher, I marched my students in lockstep fashion through chapter after chapter, assigning reading and stock questions almost every night. They had little choice about anything because I was intent on "covering" the material as quickly as possible. Some brainstorming at a faculty meeting might surface dozens of ways various teachers provide a choice for today's iGen'ers. For students used to plenty of choices every time they pick up their cell phones, regimentation and a lack of choice when they get to Mrs. McGillicuty's classroom does little to engage and interest them.

Build a Better Classroom with Choice

Social media may be a great way to connect quickly with lots of teachers who are currently providing choices for their students at every grade level. In addition to Telannia Norfar's norms for a successful and smooth-running math class, here are a few other opportunities to put brainstorming to use in classrooms:

- Listening skills are crucial when it comes to communicating and collaborating in classrooms. Students could brainstorm a list of such skills (paraphrasing, asking questions to provide clarity, supportive body language, using correctly pronounced names, and more) that students can discuss and practice all year long.

- Speaking skills are also an essential part of communication and collaboration; students could brainstorm a list of speaking skills

CHAPTER 2

(in-control gestures, speaking clearly and not too quickly, pausing for emphasis or allowing listeners to process new information, and more), then discuss and practice them throughout the year. (Oral language skills are critical to success when it comes to making project-based learning presentations.)

- Students could brainstorm a list of possible topics for reports or term papers.

- Students can brainstorm and chart a list of questions pertaining to a topic just discussed, then choose two or three to answer for homework.

- One teacher has her students read silently every day, and they may pick their own books. She may assign books within a certain genre, but students still have choices as to the titles.

CHAPTER 3
"BUT I TOLD THEM!"

There are classrooms where the procedures teachers have decreed are listed on laminated posters for all to see, but the list has become invisible to students. I have seen lesson plans that state clearly what is supposed to happen, but what actually happens bears no relation to the plan. The plan breaks down when students are not sure what to do, where to go, or how to proceed. This causes no small amount of frustration for teachers who raise their hands to the ceiling in the faculty lounge and say to no one in particular, "But I told them!" Anyone with a teenager living under their roof may well recognize the angst on the part of teachers who know what they want students to do, but look on in amazement when things go awry when it comes to process.

I ask you to forget content for a moment, something that is hard to do because that is why we are all here, isn't it? *I teach science for heaven's sake; I shouldn't have to teach students how to understand and deliver on process-related matters.* "I told them!" is no doubt what one parent said to another when taking out the trash or feeding the dog seems to be a bridge—or a request—too far. One teacher told me it was his job to deliver the information; if they didn't get it, that was not his problem. It was, as he saw it, his job to "tell them."

My father loved baseball, but he and I arrived early at the conclusion that I was not going to be a home run hero. Doubles and triples were out of the question. He worked with me on making contact and turning me into a singles hitter. I can't remember if he made a laminated poster to remind me of what to do to make that happen, but I do remember we worked every day on putting the bat on the ball in a way that, in maybe one time at bat out of four, got me to first base. Perfect practice, said the

CHAPTER 3

famous and successful football coach Vince Lombardi, makes perfect. I don't know about the perfect part, but I did okay in Little League as a singles hitter. Had my father not attended to process, I would have spent a whole lot more time on the bench.

Classroom teachers need to decide before school starts what to do with the first days and weeks of school as it relates to procedures. Posters may look good, but practice, practice, practice in classrooms is the location, location, and location of real estate. In one elementary school, the hallways were quiet and orderly for the simple reason that every teacher in the school had their students practice walking down the hallways so as not to disturb classes—and teachers who used to dread the sound of feet—and voices—in the hallway could count on silence. The teachers, by the way, came up with that solution. It worked because they made it work. Consistency when it comes to classroom procedures benefits students as well as teachers.

Students who may have problems with a particular subject don't need to deal with process issues on a regular basis. Darcy Cupp, an eighth-grade math teacher at Skyline Middle School in Front Royal, Virginia, begins to turn procedures into routines on the first day of school. She understands that providing structure when it comes to process helps everyone, most of all students who may have a problem with math content. For example, each class begins with a warm-up activity, and on day one in August, Cupp has them practice exactly what she wants them to do. She has them leave the room and enter again and again until they have the warm-up routine down. "I am consistent on holding my students to these processes every time we do them in class," says Cupp. Every process (working in groups, desk work, etc.) receives the same treatment, and students are quick to let her know they appreciate the consistency (personal communication, April 4, 2019).

There are teachers who want to hit the ground running with content, and they may wind up hitting the wall if their procedures are not in place and functioning within the first few weeks of school. Every teacher will probably agree that time is of the essence in classrooms with precious little of that commodity. Yet I have observed in classrooms where procedures have not become routine, something that can lead to all sorts of problems for teachers and their students. Students who take three minutes to get into standing pairs for a conversation are wasting time. Teachers who put up with slow transitions of any kind are themselves wasting time. Most students want things to run smoothly in their classrooms; they will be disappointed when teachers allow the process train to derail time after time.

Building a Better Classroom with Routines

When I observe a classroom where the teacher seems to be ready to head for the exits and retire early, I can often point to inconsistencies when it comes to process. They may "know their stuff" when it comes to course content, but procedural chaos can make what the teacher knows irrelevant. Here are some processes that need attention in the first two weeks or so of school:

What is the procedure for

- bringing students back to you when they are talking or collaborating?
- sharpening a pencil?
- turning in homework?
- moving from student desks into standing pairs?
- moving from standing pairs into quartets?
- transitioning from groups back to student desks?
- cleaning up and lining up (elementary) before leaving the room?
- cleaning up after a science lab?
- choosing partners for group work?

The next—and equally important—questions are these:

- How will you create routines out of the procedures you know well, but about which they haven't a clue at this point?
- What will you do when the routines that seemed efficient break down over time? (Answer: Practice it again until the procedure has become a routine.)

CHAPTER 4
CONGRUENCE

Great communicators like Winston Churchill, John F. Kennedy, and Martin Luther King, Jr., asserts Allen (2014), connected with audiences because, *every aspect of their delivery* was communicating the same message. Their choice of words, tone of voice, pacing, use of pauses, eye contact, and physical gestures were all focused on that key idea. The term used to describe this effect is *congruence*. Allen goes on to say that "while we don't have to teach everything at the level of intensity these speakers demonstrated, we can occasionally use congruence to reinforce key points of information—like directions" (p. 53).

Allen says these three things should be congruent when giving directions in classrooms:

1. Our tone of voice must support the fact that we are giving directions—don't shout—but be authoritative.

2. Our hand gestures must add clarity—demonstrate the circle you're asking your students to make; hold up fingers to reinforce numbers; point in the direction you want them to move.

3. Our body language must further emphasize the idea—turn your body in the direction they must go to get a handout; lean to one side if they must lean over to talk with another student; walk toward the door if everyone is heading to another room. (p. 53)

CHAPTER 4

Having set up my laptop on a desk in a corner of a high school classroom, I watched students enter the room, chat with friends, get out some materials, and begin to settle in and settle down. The only thing missing when it was time to begin was the teacher. She was in the hallway, chatting with a colleague well past the ringing of the late bell. The students continued to chat, too, in a way that told me this was all entirely normal in that classroom, even expected.

But the kicker was this: On the wall was a list of the teacher's rules, one of which informed students in large, bold type that they had better be on time for class. There were others, of course, but as I glanced at the laminated list in a prominent place, I was struck by the difference between what it said and what I saw happen. Then I remembered that there were students who came in late as well, and I deduced that this, too, was normal. The list of norms was an unreliable witness. The *reality* was what no doubt played out every day in a class that began with incongruent behavior on the part of the teacher.

Walking into one's own classroom a minute or so late may seem like a small thing, but the message it sends to students is one of incongruence. The action is not consistent with the stated expectations. A teacher who promises he will get test papers back within three days and does not come through consistently has moved into the land of incongruence as well. The teacher who has a wall poster that tells students they should treat each other with respect, then proceeds to yell at her students, sends a message that is unfortunate on so many levels. The teacher who tells band members she will be at the concert, then forgets to attend, is sending the wrong message.

The teacher who is consistently late might as well take down the poster that exhorts students to be on time. The teacher who does not return quizzes, tests, or other assignments on time can't complain when students are late with their homework or projects. The bottom line here is that teachers ought to demonstrate congruent behavior beginning on day one. The old do-as-I-do principle applies here. Students, I have learned over the years, are nothing if not perceptive. They know when there is a lack of congruent behavior on the part of the person who made up the existing set of rules or norms to begin with, then posted them for all to see.

Teachers can help build a better classroom by working on the kind of self-awareness that can help catch inconsistencies as they occur. They can also take the time at regular intervals to solicit feedback from students. In addition to stating the rules and explaining classroom norms intended to make for a smooth-running classroom, teachers can also lead a whole-class discussion concerning the importance of congruence not only in the classroom, but in life. That discussion is best held during the first week of school, maybe on the first day. Students want to know teachers will follow up, follow through, and walk the talk.

Building a Better Classroom with Congruence

Take a look at your classroom rules and norms and ask these questions:

- In what ways can I demonstrate congruent behavior?
- What should I do when I don't?
- How could I get feedback from students concerning my consistency when it comes to the rules, norms, or anything else?
- What could I gain from talking about all of this with a colleague or group of colleagues?
- At the beginning of the year, can students help come up with a list of norms for students—and the teacher?

CHAPTER 5
THE FEAR FACTOR

Fear is useful for humans. If I want to make a left-hand turn across traffic and I'm not able to see what is coming in the outside lane, my limbic system kicks in and informs me that staying right where I am for now is a really good idea. Fear keeps us from doing something stupid, but it also works against us when we are faced with risks in the classroom, and this applies to teachers as well as students. The eighth grader who doesn't want to appear dumb in front of his peers doesn't answer a question in class, even though he's pretty sure he knows the answer. The teacher who has become comfortable with the status quo in her classroom may be afraid to experiment or otherwise take risks in the name of improvement for her students.

The fear of making a mistake keeps students from contributing, asking or answering questions, and otherwise taking part in the proceedings during a whole-class discussion. Yet mistakes are an essential part of the learning process. We need to let students know up front, and in every classroom, that making mistakes is perfectly okay. Anderson (2019) puts this in a way that should make teachers—and students—nod their heads in agreement:

> We would never try to set up a model of teaching academics where students aren't supposed to make mistakes. Mispronouncing words is part of learning to read. Misplaying notes is a natural part of learning to play an instrument. Trying science experiments that don't come out the way we expect is a necessary part of the scientific process. If students work on math problems without making mistakes, they're almost certainly not growing as mathematicians. (p. 59)

CHAPTER 5

Every bit of what Anderson says makes perfect sense, yet I hear teachers offer criticism in place of positive and useful feedback when something is wrong. Things are supposed to go wrong. In my books and presentations, I often talk about my experience as a bagger, cashier, and stocker in a supermarket. The opportunities for mistakes were simply too numerous to count—or avoid. Yet when I made a whopper of a mistake when it came to ordering groceries from the wholesaler, the owner/manager confessed to making bigger mistakes when he first started in the grocery business. When mistakes are obvious, there is no need to do much more than move on. When our band director in college heard a mistake during band practice, there was no need to point, shout, or otherwise embarrass the malefactor. He simply said, "Let's begin again at G." Corrective action was taken, and we all moved on. Mistakes were expected and in difficult pieces of music that were more complex than some, mistakes were bound to be legion, but it was understood that this was the case.

We should want students to take risks in school, but very often they will take the easiest courses so that they can maintain that straight A standing and wind up on the stage accepting the award as valedictorian or salutatorian. This kind of success "can build a fragile foundation," write Farson and Keyes in *Whoever Makes the Most Mistakes Wins: The Paradox of Innovation* (2002). "Those not tested by setbacks when young may never learn how to rebound from defeat" (p. 51). The comfortable path through school may not serve the students who take it—and the parents who encourage them to do so because of the awards that accompany a diploma on graduation day. "The only problem with success," said Tommy Lasorda, "is that it does not teach you how to deal with failure" (Farson and Keyes, p. 55).

One of the reasons I like project-based learning is that it provides students with the opportunities to experiment, collaborate, research, make—and deal with—mistakes along the way, and ask questions for the best of all reasons, to discover and understand things. Young kids ask questions in bunches, *and it is because they are curious*. If we are providing students with experiences in school that matter to them, they will be curious no matter their age. The problem with traditional classrooms is that teachers often discourage questions because time is short and the textbook is long. But this shortchanges students who might otherwise take their curiosity to levels they abandoned somewhere along the way to middle school.

Wagner and Dintersmith (2015) lament the fact that we are obsessed with finding new ways to help students excel when it comes to standardized tests, but we don't give them the skills they need in the innovation age in which we now live. One of the things the authors point out is that students involved in doing research online "can become experts in days, not weeks or years. They can find online the most compelling essays, lectures, videos, and forums. They can ask 'dumb' questions without risk of embarrassment" (197). Asking questions is a great learning tool, but students in traditional classroom settings are often afraid of the kind of embarrassment that will put them in a bad light in front of their peers. If everyone is asking questions, "dumb" or otherwise, doing so is the norm, not the exception.

The biggest worry for students in classrooms may well be the way classmates react to a wrong answer, an incomplete answer, an inarticulate answer or question, an obvious grammatical mistake when speaking in class, or, and this happened to me on at least one memorable occasion in high school, the realization that the teacher just asked for an answer to a question the student did not hear. Teachers cannot accept or condone rude behavior on the part of anyone in the classroom. Accepting rude or otherwise inappropriate behavior is asking for trouble—and an escalation of such conduct.

Teachers also want to avoid embarrassing students. My experience is that doing so raises the level of fear in classrooms exponentially, especially when it is done *deliberately* by a teacher. Humiliation is not a tool. "When correcting a student," write Curwin, Mendler, and Mendler (2018), "pause and put yourself at the receiving end of what you are about to say. If it would embarrass you, it will probably embarrass him" (p. 100–101). When a teacher embarrasses a student, an apology should be heartfelt and immediate. "Forgive yourself for not being perfect, then find a time to genuinely apologize" (Curwin, Mendler, and Mendler, 2018, p. 101). Having embarrassed a student in one of my classes, I immediately apologized, then called the parent that evening.

CHAPTER 5

IF YOU CAN'T MAKE A MISTAKE... YOU CAN'T MAKE ANYTHING

Build a Better Classroom by Banishing Fear in Classrooms

A heaping dose of empathy is probably the best way to banish fear from classrooms, and I have come to believe that this is so important a topic that it deserves a good deal of collaboration on the part of administrators and teachers who can share knowledge, experience, and the research; brainstorm ways to keep classrooms emotionally safe; and continually revisit this topic every year in some fashion.

Teachers can invite a colleague they know and trust to observe a class period or, in an elementary setting, maybe thirty minutes during the course of the day, asking the visitor to look for one thing: evidence of the existence of fear on the part of students. In the course of three decades observing teachers at all grade levels, I have seen fear and unremitting tension dismantle an otherwise excellent lesson plan, even as it prevents the development of positive, constructive relationships. Teachers and administrators, working together, can send fear packing in classrooms and throughout the school, but it takes work.

CHAPTER 6
REASSURING REDUNDANCIES

On many occasions since the advent of the internet, I have seen teachers and presenters attempt to use a video clip as the centerpiece of a lesson or presentation. Their assumption is that it will work. On occasion it does not, and the teacher/presenter, after spending an inordinate amount of time trying to fix things, simply apologizes and moves on. I have observed lessons where the required graphic from a computer does not appear on the screen. In one case, I read panic on the face of a teacher who had no Plan B. In one primary classroom, the teacher told the students they should take about five minutes to cut out some geographic shapes using small scissors and construction paper with the shapes printed thereon. It took almost twenty-five minutes, and pushed the intended, all-important activity much further into the morning.

When I present in schools and districts, whenever possible I take an extra projector, an extra Bose SoundDock (I use music constantly), extra batteries of all sizes, an additional remote for the PowerPoint, and extra cords of every kind. I do this because what I don't want to do is operate in an environment free of redundancy. If something goes wrong with my equipment, I want to go to Plan B right away, without delay, and without playing the blame game: "This was working yesterday!" or "This manufacturer has some problems, that's for sure!" or "Is there a technician in the house?" I always have a Plan B, and I go with it; but I can't go with something I don't have.

Let's look at the three situations in the first paragraph. If the teacher/presenter had downloaded the clip into a presentation program and checked it out a few times, including just before the class/session, there is a high probability that Plan B will not be necessary. If a teacher who

CHAPTER 6

has as the centerpiece of a lesson a computer-based chart that will drive the work of discussion groups has also taken the time to print out a single copy, then procured an LCD projector from another teacher, he may not use it, but he has it. The teacher who simply misjudged the time it would take for third graders to cut out geographic shapes could have come to class with the shapes cut. The essential and substantive part of the lesson came *after* the shapes were ready.

In each case above, problems could have been avoided had some extra time and effort been put into Plan B. From experience, and I learned much of this the hard way, redundancies are as reassuring as they are effective. Wishing or assuming something is going to happen according to plan often results in frustration and embarrassment.

Having Plan B also means never having to say you're sorry. Apologizing does not move anything forward. All it does is alert the participants to the fact that you are not prepared for any eventuality. Accentuating the positive is the hallmark of a great teacher. Students have enough negativity in their lives; they don't need negative behavior on the part of their teachers. Framing becomes important when unfortunate and unforeseen circumstances arise.

Allen and Hann (2012) suggest that if one has an alternative plan in place, framing the problem in a positive light is superior to casting a negative pall over the proceedings. The negative approach might be stated this way:

> Oh, wow, I'm sorry guys, this is so annoying. I don't know what I'm going to do for the rest of the presentation without the projector working. But bear with me and we'll see how it goes. (p. 43)

The positive frame of the same situation might go like this, if Plan B is available:

> Good news! The data projector isn't working today, and I've been working on some new ways of exploring these concepts—without using any slides. So, this is a perfect opportunity to try them out. I'm intrigued to see how it works, because I think these alternate ways of looking at the concepts will be much more interesting and useful to you. (Allen and Hann, p. 44)

Plan B may turn out to be superior to Plan A. On occasion, the failure of my first choice of processes has led to discarding them altogether when I have determined that the alternative resulted in more engagement—and a better understanding of the concept—on the part of participants.

Built-in redundancy can alleviate suffering on your part, eliminate the need to play the blame game or apologize, reduce the amount of time to get things moving after the problem occurs, and result in your students seeing you as more credible in their eyes. Don't overlook the value of checking with colleagues to discover how *they* ensure that Plan B is always at hand. Collaboration with other teachers can result in the availability of anything any of the teachers might need. Chances are you are not the first teacher to present that lesson, use those strategies or that equipment, make a process-related mistake, or encounter a roadblock along the way. A backup plan may also be just a social media request away.

Build a Better Classroom with Redundancies

Take a look at your processes, your equipment, and your materials:

- If a process is unavailable for any reason, what will take its place?
- What is the alternative to apologizing for something that goes wrong?
- If you can't access something electronically, where is the paper version?
- If your electronic whiteboard runs amuck, where are the markers and the chart stand?
- If something you are trying is simply not working, what is the immediate alternative? What can you do to salvage the process and improve the outcomes?
- Finally, if the bulb burns out, the batteries expire, the remote dies, your computer goes offline, or your students project only confusion—how close is the remedy? How near is the redundancy? How completely prepared are you for the unexpected?
- Would a search on a social media platform offer some alternatives from colleagues to what you have planned?

CHAPTER 7
EVERYONE IN THE (LEARNING) POOL

I have found that decisions in teacher-centered classrooms (like my own back in the day) are often made based on current and future budgets, available materials, textbooks, equipment, technology, and myriad factors unrelated to the sheer joy of learning. Adults next to a community pool often scurry about in search of shade in a safe place where they won't be splashed anytime soon, but kids want nothing more than to get wet. They want to get in the pool, and they encourage everyone to join them. After all, what is the point of having a pool if the arrangement of the pool furniture is as far as our pool-related involvement goes? What kid wants to listen to lectures on the history of pools while the sun is high in the sky and the water temperature is perfect?

I have had the good fortune to observe and do a bit of coaching in hundreds of classrooms at all levels and in all subject areas over many years, and when I think of where I would want any kids of mine to be, it is in the classrooms where everyone, teachers and students alike, is in the pool—the learning pool—together. Budgets will intrude from time to time, materials are updated—or not, equipment works—or it doesn't, and technology adds immeasurably to the proceedings. But as I think back on my visits to the best classrooms, teachers and students are all partners in learning. Those teachers still consider themselves as students, and the students relish the fact that their teachers are in the learning pool with them, splashing, laughing, jostling, and learning.

Greeted at the door by a junior in a high school science class, I followed him into a classroom lost in learning. No one at the lectern. No one giving orders. No one dispensing knowledge from the front of the room. The student who had met me at the door showed me his portfolio, an impressive and lengthy document that clearly demonstrated his progress over time. Four or five minutes into the class, I still had not met the teacher. The room was a hotbed of collaboration and cooperation between and among students and groups. Students sought each other's help and feedback during the entire time I was in the classroom.

When she had a moment, the teacher introduced herself to me and explained that failure was not an option in that science classroom. Feedback came from every direction, and continuous improvement was their mantra. She told me her aha moment came when she realized she wasn't the only teacher in the room, and I concluded that they were not the only students. They were in the learning pool together, and it was a joyful thing to watch.

Students want to know that their teachers are passionate about what they do, and when teachers reveal themselves as lifelong learners, this sets a great example for students. When I first started teaching, I thought my job was to impart in the classroom what I had learned in four years of college. My students did not see in me someone who is still learning and excited about doing so: "To students," says Fried (2001),

> teachers are critically important role models because of what they are still learning, not just because of what they already know. It is as experienced learners, with a high interest in and high standards for knowledge and skills, that we communicate the lasting value of these things to students.

Absent that passion for learning, we become "purveyors of subject matter," adds Fried (p. 25), something I must admit described my early classrooms. I imparted information to the multitudes in a largely passive and teacher-centered environment.

Every teacher has a decision to make. Is this classroom going to be an adult-centered, largely passive environment, or will it be learner-centered, with the learner-in-chief taking an integral part in the proceedings? Risk-taking is an integral component of a robust and highly successful learning environment. An adult-centered classroom can operate remarkably free of risk on the part of every human within the four walls. Students, as affirmed by Frey, Fisher, and Smith (2019), need to build identity and agency, the former being "the narrative we tell the world and ourselves about ourselves." Agency "describes our capacity to act in empowered and autonomous ways" (p. 20). In the passive, largely static world of the adult-centered classroom, the development of identity and agency is not possible. Pretending to listen while taking a few notes, watching a filmstrip or video, and filling in the blanks on successive worksheets build little except resentment over time.

Almarode and Miller (2018) compare surface-level learners to snorkelers, and they compare deep-level learners with scuba divers. Adult-centered classrooms operate on the surface, while learner-centered classrooms open the ocean depths to discovery—and more risk on the part of the learners. Shifting from a sage-on-the-stage approach to a more learner-centered classroom culture involves risk on the part of teachers often steeped in tradition: "Changing our own practice is successful," write Almarode and Miller, "only when we reflect on our own journey from snorkeling to scuba diving and, along with our students, see ourselves as learners" (p. 163). My experience as I visit classrooms is that students who are allowed to be students are happy campers who are glad to have teachers in the learning pool with them.

Teachers can learn much by talking with, sharing with, teaching with, and working with colleagues. As we'll see in chapter 49, reflective teaching is more powerful when it is done in a collaborative fashion and based on evidence of student progress (DuFour, 2015). My most successful and satisfying years in the classroom came as a member of an inclusion team, and we grew together as teachers in ways each of us working alone would not have been able to do. Teams of teachers working together generate ideas and excitement, and they get results. I find that teams of teachers asked to share what it is they are doing fall over each other as they describe their efforts and successes on behalf of kids. They are quick to show the data and discuss the feedback from students and parents. They are full of energy in a way that often eludes teachers who have been teaching in the same classrooms for a dozen years and hesitate to share or work with other teachers because that involves considerable risk, and risk aversion can be a constant companion for teachers mired in the status quo—and afraid to get in the pool.

CHAPTER 7

Build Better Classrooms by Becoming Learning Partners with Students

Part of learning is making mistakes and unforced errors. Take a moment on occasion to admit your own mistakes and failures, and let students know those inevitable speed bumps are simply part of the continuous improvement process. What often stands in the way of moving forward for students is a fear of taking risks that come with being outside their comfort zones. Talk about that with them. Explain the concept of learning when we take risks and are, therefore, no longer hanging on to the status quo.

Here are some questions you might have students discuss in standing pairs:

- Why is failure part of the learning process?
- What mistakes have you made that helped you grow as a learner?
- What can we learn from each other as learning partners?
- What can we learn from the perspectives of others?
- Why is tackling new information made easier in pairs or groups?

CHAPTER 8
THE LIGHTER SIDE

Today's test-driven educational system places enormous stress on students, administrators at all levels, and teachers. The resultant pressure causes teachers and administrators no little discomfort in anticipation of the test results. I have seen the faculty members of a school that was not accredited sit glumly while other schools receive accolades not available to them during this district-wide celebration. Students move from one classroom to another, carrying with them emotional baggage they can't seem to shake, at least not in the passive climate of many classrooms where they successfully block what is on offer academically in favor of whatever is bugging them on this Monday morning.

We overload students with assignments, says Abeles (2015), "when the key to learning is new experiences" (p. 37). A teacher's workmanlike approach to learning may reflect the pressure he or she feels to have their students perform on standardized tests. Students feel that pressure, and "excessive stress isn't doing much for children's intellectual strength," asserts Abeles (p. 36). However, when students are deeply engaged in their own learning and surrounded by classmates and teachers who are learning right along with them, intellectual growth is possible, new friendships are formed, and there is little time to brood or watch the clock. "Emotions are central for learning," writes Posey (2019, p. 8), and there are many things teachers can do to help shift students from stress-filled moods to happier places where meaningful engagement and learning become the norm.

One way to lift moods is, as we'll see in chapter 34, through the use of upbeat music. Music is a mood lifter, and my experience is that when students—or adults—enter a classroom or any presentation venue to the sounds of lively music, they start out in a better place. I played

CHAPTER 8

"My Girl," by The Temptations, years ago in an auditorium with about 350 new teachers (and teachers new to the district, most of whom were Baby Boomers or Gen Xers), and before we were one verse into the song, everyone in that auditorium was singing along and swaying from side to side in unison. I just turned off the music and let them have at it. That happened a minute or so into the presentation, and it set the tone for the next three hours.

Another way to lighten the mood is through the use of running gags. I mispronounced a word in one of my history classes, which resulted in a great deal of laughter on the part of everyone in the room, including me. I ran with that mistake for the rest of the class period. The fact that I could laugh at myself—and at my unforced errors—somehow made me more human to my seventh graders. This happened in other classes periodically, and always with the same result. Comedians have great success with running gags, and there is no reason why teachers can't do the same thing. I always suggest that teachers lighten up a bit and have some fun at their own expense. As long as everyone is laughing *with* you, go along for the ride.

Humor puts students in a better place for learning. Toxic learning environments have the opposite effect. Saying, as I did on many occasions, "Pay attention now. This is on the test!" probably didn't lift any moods; I've never been sure what paying attention is, but threatening students with Friday's quiz or test is not the best way to put them in learning mode. But I can still remember storylines from Dr. Haines, my favorite history professor in college, who infused humor of all kinds into his stories of Tudor and Stuart luminaries (along with the not-so-famous) of sixteenth- and seventeenth-century Britain. His hour-long classes were among the very few I hated to see come to an end during my undergraduate days. In fact, the professors I remember—and enjoyed—the most had this in common: They had a great sense of humor, never took themselves too seriously, and were not afraid to laugh at themselves.

I'm not suggesting, by the way, that teachers need to be stand-up comics or pull rabbits out of hats in their classrooms. But teachers are human, and human frailties provide us with stories we can tell about those things that happened to us. Totally shifting gears with storytelling from the professional to the personal can serve to get the attention of everyone in the room. A personal story totally unrelated to the subject material can, I have found, help students subsequently focus on the material if the story is interesting and/or humorous. Making fun of our own mistakes can send the message that making mistakes is normal, even among teachers.

Build a Better Classroom by Changing Physical and Mental States

Teachers who strive to lift moods with music, induce laughter, shift gears, and otherwise change the mental and physical state of students will find them much more attentive and receptive to new information and to whatever activities are on offer for them. The brain loves novelty. "Things to which we are accustomed," writes Tate (2012), "become mundane and require little special attention" (p. 136). New and pleasant experiences serve to help us focus.

When I am presenting to adults, here are some things I do regularly to change the mental and physical states of participants:

- While they are entering the presentation venue, upbeat music is always playing.

- Before we begin, I ask them to find a writing instrument, lift it high, and compliment several neighbors on their writing instruments, to the accompaniment of more upbeat music. (I learned this from a fifth-grade teacher years ago, and it serves two purposes: It creates laughter and movement, and it determines who does and does not have a writing instrument. There is truly method in the madness.)

- I frequently have participants stand and pair up somewhere in the room, then move with that partner into quartets, then move back into pairs, then go back to their seats—again, to the accompaniment of upbeat music.

- Before participants stand in preparation for a bit of sharing, I display some humor on the screen. (For example: "What do your mom and dad have in common?" An eight-year-old's

CHAPTER 8

answer: "They both don't want any more kids.") The movement and the laughter release dopamine, which allows participants to focus.

A word of caution when it comes to the use of humor: sarcasm is not funny when directed at someone, anyone. I once had a prospective substitute teacher tell me she thought sarcasm and humiliation were good classroom management tools. In a sidebar conversation, I gently disabused her of that notion. "Emotional safety is undermined by sarcasm, impatience and contempt," affirms Bluestein (2001), and "by teachers who yell or humiliate" (p. 3). The great teachers I have come to know over the years understand that sarcasm, humiliation, and gargantuan temper tantrums have no place in schools. Moods are not lightened by any of those actions; tension is created or *increased* by such behavior, which should not be tolerated between and among students, either.

Here are some questions you can ask yourself or share with a colleague:

- Are there interesting and humorous stories about myself I can share with students?
- Are there humorous anecdotes about the subject matter that can be shared?
- What kind of humor is totally *inappropriate*?
- How will I react when students use sarcasm and/or humiliation against classmates?
- How can I change the physical or mental state of my students to get them ready for whatever comes next?

CHAPTER 9
"YOU IN THE YELLOW SHIRT!"

When I am setting up a presentation at the school or district level, I request a table just outside the entrance to the workshop venue. On that table, I place several black markers and enough blank stick-on name tags for everyone. I do this in part because many years ago, I attended a workshop where the facilitator neglected to do this; when someone raised his or her hand, the facilitator identified the would-be responder with something akin to, "Yes. No, not you, the man in the yellow shirt. That's right." I have also been in classrooms at the secondary level where it is obvious after a few minutes of classroom discourse that the teacher either does not know everyone's name or simply chooses not to use them, even though it is October.

"Names," writes Mike Anderson (2019), "are part of who we are. They give us a sense of self-worth and power" (p. 31). Teachers who take a long time to learn the names of their students, or, worse, don't bother to memorize them at all, are disrespecting those students. By contrast, those teachers who make an effort to learn students' names—and pronounce them correctly—demonstrate respect in a way the students appreciate. I always recommend elementary teachers learn the names of their students on the first day of school, and use them frequently during the first week. For secondary teachers with well over a hundred students spread over several classes, memorizing names on the first day is a stretch, but learning them in the first week or so is not. Lots of mini conversations when conferencing with students in the classroom, between classes, before and after school starts, at lunch, or after school give teachers opportunities to use names over and over again.

CHAPTER 9

If I ask a seminar participant about the correct pronunciation of his or her name, I invariably hear, "Thank you for asking that," or words to the like effect. This tells me what I already know: Others have mispronounced—often badly—that person's name, no doubt on many occasions. Once I learn the correct pronunciation of the name, I stay with that person for a minute or so, using the name three or four times, including just before I walk away. On my way to my next stop (as I introduce myself to participants), I use the name I just learned several more times. When her hand goes up during a whole-class segment, or when I stop beside a pair or group of conversationalists that includes her, I can ask her something *and use her name in the process*. I have seen people with a name that is difficult to pronounce display a beaming smile when I use it correctly an hour or two into the session.

Anderson (2019) provides some strategies for learning names:

- Have students wear name tags for the first two weeks of school.
- Use students' names as often as possible early in the year.
- Practice remembering students' names in your head during your commute.
- Encourage students to use each other's names in class. (p. 32)

This last suggestion is particularly important. I recommend that when teachers put students in seated or standing pairs, they be required to use the names of their partners, and this can be modeled: "So, what did you think of the story, Martha." If students are going to build a sense of community in the classroom, using names and pronouncing them correctly is paramount. It demonstrates respect for classmates, which is necessary if students are to communicate and collaborate effectively.

Building a Better Classroom by Learning Names Quickly

Here are some suggestions when it comes to memorizing the names of students and at the same time letting them know you understand the importance of correctly spelled and pronounced names to all of us:

- When students are entering or leaving your classroom, place yourself at the door, and use their names as they pass by.
- When you first meet a student, engage him in a short conversation, using his name several times in the process. When you walk away, use his name again silently.
- As you are learning the names of students during the first hours or days of school, use their names frequently as you call on them or take questions: "Yes, Marcia. Give us your question." Then, "Thanks, Marcia, for sharing." Later: "Remember what Marcia said a few minutes ago," or "Bob, I think you are building on what Marcia contributed just now."
- Consider putting students in standing pairs and have them discuss with a partner why our names are important to us. Once students are back in their seats, brainstorm a bit, listing the reasons on the whiteboard or on a piece of chart paper. (I recommend chart paper; you can tear off the sheet from the pad and place it on the wall for a couple of days as a reminder of just why you—and they—should take the time to memorize and use names.)
- If you have them wear name tags, explain that this will make it easier for you and all their classmates to learn and use names beginning on the first day of school. (Name tents on desks are fine for you, but when students stand and talk with one another, the tents don't go with them.)
- If you have a personal story about someone you know whose name was difficult to pronounce, you can share that story as a door opener into the importance of memorizing names and taking the time to learn and use the correct pronunciation.
- Students will sometimes make fun of names. Whether it is names in a textbook, a story, or from a video they have just seen, teachers need to nip that in the bud. Sometimes it is necessary to call a time-out and discuss what is accepted behavior and what is not. Students are often sensitive about their own names, and when a classmate makes fun of a name in any context, it resonates immediately with those students whose names are difficult to pronounce or just different.

CHAPTER 10
TRIGGER THE CALM

I had students who seemed to have located, and stepped on, my last nerve. On several occasions, as I recall, that last nerve often left the classroom on the bottom of some student's shoe or sneaker. I sometimes failed to respond in a calm and positive way to willful misbehavior or to negative comments or sarcasm on the part of students. The result of losing my temper (or responding to sarcasm with more sarcasm) was always less than satisfying and often more than a bit damaging. I once apologized to a student and the entire class for losing it. I had responded loudly and in a decidedly negative fashion to something the student said. Not exactly cool, calm, and collected on that—and other—occasions.

Fred Jones (2014) points out that what we all learned in biology as the fight-flight reflex can be "the teacher's immediate and automatic response to goofing off" (p. 160). Jones adds that the fight-flight reflex, as with all reflexes, "is *immediate* and *automatic*. You do not choose to have it." Natural teachers, says Jones, "just manage stress more effectively" (p. 160). Jones came up with a great phrase for that inappropriate, immediate, and ultimately ineffective response to student misbehavior, called *Nag, Nag, Nag*. A couple of examples: "All right class, there is no excuse for all of this talking! When I look up, I expect to see people working!" and "Would the two of you keep your hands to yourselves and pay attention to what is going on in class? If I see any more of this behavior, you will see me after the bell" (pp. 162–163).

I used those two responses, or variations thereof, more than a few times as a young teacher. What Jones calls *squawking* and *flapping* (wild gesticulations with our arms and hands) is a tried-and-true reaction to stress that I have both seen and used on occasion. I could squawk and flap

43

with the best of them, always in ways that proved nonproductive and, as Jones points out, unnecessary.

We do our thinking in the cortex of our brains, but when we react badly to something Eddie just did or said, we downshift from our cortex into the brainstem and often lose our temper. Jones reminds us that emotions are, in fact, contagious: "If you are calm, you will have a calming effect on those around you. If you are upset, you will tend to upset those around you" (p. 168). Trigger the calm in your students by remaining calm yourself.

One tried-and-true way for teachers to control their tempers is to take a deep breath and pause before saying anything. And "squawking and flapping" does nothing but tell students the teacher is out of control. Once again, we come back to the value of building teacher-to-student relationships. Bluestein (2010) puts it succinctly: "Your relationship with your students is the vehicle through which all other goals are achieved" (p. 167). Teachers who attempt to simply control the behavior of students without building solid working relationships are headed for trouble—and quickly. Excellent rapport is key.

Build a Better Classroom by Building Rapport Over Time

In classrooms where discipline problems are few, there is one common thread that is obvious to the observer: considerable rapport between and among students and teachers has been developed over time. It is difficult, says Gershon (2018), "to foster rapport without a sense that you are truly interested in the wellbeing and goals of your students" (p. 112). As one of two members of a central office team working on organizational development for the district, I took part in interviews of forty-eight fifth graders who told us that they felt part of a family on their three-teacher team. The rapport was wide and deep; students offered that they looked out for each other and did not hesitate to help each other every day. They spoke in glowing terms of their teachers, whom they said *had their best interests at heart*. One result of the relationship building that was constantly tended to by the teachers is that they did not write a single office referral during the course of that year or in the several years following.

Teachers who take the time to establish excellent relationships with students are much more credible in their eyes. Kohn (2006) affirms,

> Educators who form truly caring relationships with students are not only meeting emotional needs; they are also setting a powerful example. Whenever an adult listens patiently, or shows concern for someone he doesn't know, or apologizes for something he regrets having said, he is modeling for students, teaching them how they might be with each other. (p. 113)

Because building relationships in classrooms is so important, and because there are teachers who have mastered the art of establishing great rapport with and among students, I suggest teachers find those colleagues and then make the time (inside or outside the school day) to discuss rapport-building techniques:

- What works for them in terms of building solid relationships?
- How do they set the stage at the beginning of the school year for their success in building rapport?
- Could new teachers visit the classrooms of teachers who have excellent rapport with their students?
- If we want students to build rapport with one another, what role does modeling play?
- What does an effective and ongoing level of *student-to-student* rapport look like? How can we get there?
- What resources and research can be located and tapped that could provide guidance and research that might assist us?

WHEN TENSION GOES UP, RETENTION GOES DOWN

CHAPTER 11
MODEL AND TEACH EFFECTIVE LISTENING SKILLS

The skills necessary to be an active and empathetic listener are not handed out at birth. And, as a new teacher, I understood that my job was as the CIO (Chief Information Officer)—the great disseminator of knowledge. My students were primarily responsible for listening. I wanted them to listen so they could take good notes. I wanted them to take good notes so they could study them and produce grades I could record in my gradebook. To me, that was how it had been in my career as a student, and, for all I knew, how it had been from the first time somebody put desks in straight rows. I had a speech class in college, but listening classes weren't in the course catalog.

In highly interactive and student-centered classrooms, conversations between students in pairs and groups are frequent, and once students are comfortable combining the roles of speaker and listener, teachers can move them in the direction of academic conversations. Zwiers (2020) asserts that we need to work at being good listeners. The problem is that "we tend to value what *we* think and say over what others are thinking and saying" (p.65). We can help students become better listeners. For example, as we'll explore in chapter 39, when one student in a pair is finished speaking, the listener can paraphrase what the speaker said in search of understanding; he or she can challenge what the speaker said; he or she can build on what the speaker said; and he or she can add new ideas to the conversation as together they build understanding.

When students share in whole-class settings, teachers can model good listening skills. It is sometimes difficult for students to share anything in front of thirty classmates, and teachers can facilitate each student's contributions to discussions by modeling empathy. One empathy-related

CHAPTER 11

skill involves not judging fellow students. "Some students," says Costa (2008), "ridicule, laugh at, or put down other students' ideas" (p. 33). Teachers need to model what to do when ideas are presented: accept them unconditionally. Everyone in the room should know how to react—or not to react—when a student contributes something aloud. In junior high school, I watched as one of my classmates was humiliated by her fellow students because she lacked the information that would have kept her from responding to a question the way she did. It was devastating for her.

When a student—any student, shy or otherwise—shares something with the class, I recommend teachers thank them for sharing in a quick, simple way: "Thank you for sharing, Monica." Notice the use of Monica's name (something that honors students). Also, I have seen teachers respond in an over-the-top manner when Reggie, who *never* contributes out loud, does so. The teacher is so startled—not to mention ecstatic—that she does everything up to and including bringing out the brass bands, cheerleaders, and a bag or two of confetti. This unnecessary display winds up embarrassing a student who would have been quite happy with the same thank-you everyone else normally gets. I also recommend the use of the command voice, rather than an approachable voice, when thanking students for sharing. This is a steady, calm voice (not a sing-song voice) that drops off slightly at the end. Try it: "Thank you for sharing, Connie."

On occasion, several students will raise their hands to say something, and all of those hands need to be recognized. Here is an idea that will keep things flowing smoothly, even as student input is acknowledged. When four hands go up, say the following: "Mary, I'll take your question first, followed by Stan, Melissa, and Yolanda. Hands down. Thanks. Mary?" This obviates the need for the uncalled-on students to keep their hands waving frenetically, lest the teacher ignore them. The key here is to make sure you remember the other three names, and in order. This takes practice, I have found, but it honors everyone without keeping the distraction caused by all those waving hands at bay.

I once watched as a middle school teacher said, after one of her students responded to an open-ended question, "Thank you for sharing, Todd. What more could we add to what Todd just said?" What I remember is how Todd (not his real name) reacted to this. He sat up a little straighter. His teacher had accepted his input, then turned to his classmates to build on it. She was saying that what he said had value, and that the rest of his peers ("What more could *we* add . . . ?") were now free to expand Todd's thought. Good listeners look to build on the buzz.

Another way to show someone you are listening is to seek clarity. *What you are saying is important, and I want to get it straight. I want to see if I understand it.* Paraphrasing and asking a clarifying question are two powerful listening skills. Once again, you want to honor—and demonstrate for students how *they* can honor—not just the stuff and substance of the contribution, *but the brave soul who put it out there.* Again, the idea here is to let kids know that what they have to say and contribute is important by choosing to react in ways that prove that to them—and to the entire class. Students are nothing if not perceptive, and they see how others are treated. They process what they see and hear quickly, and their conclusions can lead them in one of two directions: *I'm willing to participate* or *I'm going to head for the mental exits now.*

Build a Better Classroom by Modeling Good Listening Skills

Finally, and I'll cover this in more detail in chapter 12, silence is a powerful tool in the learning process. But teachers are often reluctant to allow students time to think and reflect independently in class. I have found that teachers want to fill silent periods of time with their own voices. Yet we all need frequent reflective moments to sort things out and think things through, and teachers need to train themselves *to use silence as a thinking tool after a question is asked or answered.* Some students grasp the point or the meaning right away; others struggle to do so, and they need a bit of extra time. *And they need to come to understand that the teacher's default behavior is to allow that time.* They need to be able to count on it—and you.

Here are a few ideas related to modeling listening skills:

- In whole-class discussions, practice using a few seconds of wait time before responding to a question or comment from a student. One of my favorite presenters turns his head to one side for a few seconds, then turns his head back to face the group as he responds.

CHAPTER 11

- During the first days of school, whole-class and paired discussions can center on non-academic, personal subjects where students feel comfortable responding. This allows teachers to model and practice good listening skills.

- One teacher and I modeled paraphrasing skills with fifth graders, using the topic of "our favorite meal." Then we had them practice paraphrasing using the same topic. Two adults can model listening skills in front of students as well.

- The body language of speakers and listeners should be consistent with what they are saying. Sweeping gestures and the pointing of fingers in paired discussions will simply distract from the proceedings. Again, teachers can model the use of body language in paired or group discussions.

CHAPTER 12
THE BEST IS (OFTEN) SILENCE

As a teacher back in the day, I could talk with the best of them and out-talk the rest of them. I thought, apparently, that my students hung on every word. Or maybe they were just trying to hang in there as best they could, smiling at me occasionally as they mentally mulled over what clothes they were going to wear to Friday night's dance. When we studied Ancient Egypt in my world history classes, no doubt the phrase "silent as the tomb" resonated with my eighth graders. In my classroom, at least, their lot in life was to listen, or pretend to do so, while taking a few notes from the overhead projector.

It turns out that talking is not teaching after all; talking is thinking. As a teacher, I talked, therefore I thought. I thought, therefore I learned. My students sat, therefore they daydreamed, and perhaps not about Egyptian pharaohs and pyramids. In classrooms like mine, where the information consistently flows from the front of the classroom to the gathered attendees, Garrison (2016) affirms that students are "left to the imperfect task of taking accurate notes with little opportunity to think about what is being said" (p. 32). Thinking about what was said, or having students talk about what was said, requires silence on the part of the teacher. Kids need time to reflect independently, in pairs, or in small groups.

Teachers can use silence as a teaching tool while students are working in collaborative groups. As students talk and work together on small tasks or larger projects, teachers can move from group to group, listening and asking questions that answer the twin questions as they relate to their learning goals: "Where are you now related to your learning target?" and "What is your next step?" I watched as an eighth-grade science teacher

CHAPTER 12

asked those two questions to several groups—and waited patiently for the answers, asking more guided questions in the process.

In this way, listening is teaching, and as students talk their way through answers to thoughtful questions, they are thinking. Thinking is learning. The question for teachers is this: What in the way of teacher talk can be discarded in favor of student collaboration, reflection, and the asking of questions of the teacher if necessary. A student question, too, can be followed by a silence that gives others in the room or in the group a chance to mull the question over in their own minds. Rowe (1986)

> cites research that makes the case for providing adequate wait time. She concludes that "the quality of discourse can be markedly improved by increasing to 3 seconds or longer the average wait times used by teachers after a question and after a response." (cited in Nash, 2014, p. 61)

I recently watched a middle school teacher ask a question, and then wait patiently for several seconds. Sure enough, a couple of hands went up immediately. I was watching students who had their thinking caps on, then raised their hands in turn until there were perhaps a dozen or more hands in the air. Had the teacher succumbed, as I did frequently as a new teacher, to the temptation to take the first or second volunteer, those other hands would never have made it up. Worse, teachers who take the same two or three hands all the time train the rest of the students to quit thinking, because Mary and Fred are always going to process more quickly. In this classroom, however, it was obvious that adequate wait time was something the students could count on.

Build a Better Classroom with Purposeful Periods of Silence

Here are a few opportunities for silence that allow students to process a question and think about possible responses:

THE BEST IS (OFTEN) SILENCE

- Teachers can provide some wait time after asking a question or taking an answer. Multiple answers can be accepted, giving students more time to contemplate what others have said. Patience is key here.

- It is best to pause after giving one in a series of one-at-a-time directions. If the first in a series of directions was to get a writing instrument and reflective journal, pause until it is done. If you start talking before it is done, that second direction is more than likely going to be lost on many—or most—of your students.

- There is a temptation to explain a graphic or photo once it is revealed on the screen. Instead, stand to the side, look at the screen yourself (their eyes follow yours), and give them time to come to grips with what they see.

- If you display a paragraph on the screen, avoid reading it to them. If they are already reading it silently, this creates dissonance, and they may simply stop reading *and* listening. Let them read it silently while you do the same.

- If students have just read something on the screen, give them time to ponder what they have read. The same applies to a graphic or photo. If a picture is worth a thousand words, give them time to mentally form their own words and their own reaction to what they have just seen.

- If you ask your students to stop talking and face you, give everyone time to do that. If you start talking while some students are fidgeting or talking themselves, you are giving everyone permission to do the same next time.

CHAPTER 13
PRESS AND RELEASE

On a long airplane flight, I watched as a teenager across the aisle and down one row played a video game. He interacted with that video game for two hours, and I was reminded of the chatter in our faculty lounge back in the day: "These kids can't sit still! They can't concentrate!" What I observed was proof to the contrary. That young man was doing something he liked doing, and he was in continuous improvement mode. Between games, he explained to me how over the weeks he had been playing the game, he made lots of rookie mistakes that he had since corrected. He appeared to improve steadily, although the occasional groan told me he was still making mistakes, even though his rookie days were behind him. Higher *levels* of the game brought new challenges, but he was able to pause, cogitate, adjust, and begin again. He was able to *press* and *release* constantly, while doing something he found challenging but interesting.

This teenager could do on the airplane what he might not have been able to do in a classroom: He was in control of everything. He could pause when he wanted to, take a break when he needed to, and even put up with me asking questions. In classrooms, teachers often control everything, and that includes the flow of new information into working memory that can, asserts Kagan (2009), "only hold a limited amount of information. More information beyond about ten minutes is like pouring water into a glass that is already full" (p. 6.17). Yet teachers will continue to pour water all over the floor far well into the class period, and they do this because the pacing guide must be served. As a history teacher, I was particularly prone to speeding through the textbook because, well, *I was determined to get to the war in Vietnam for a change.* That textbook served as a pace-setter, and

CHAPTER 13

I pressed and pressed and pressed in an attempt to cover the material. I forgot that I was teaching students, not content. Have voice, will talk.

When we lecture for too long, we are pressing students too hard and demanding too much. They are unable to pause, ponder, and make sense of what they have heard. Worse, they may have stopped listening altogether after—or before—that ten minutes is up. One of the best ways to take the pressure off is to give students a chance to move into standing pairs and talk about what they have heard, seen, or read. One great way, affirm Allen and Scozzi (2012), is to

> make sure your students grasp core information quickly is to let them talk about it. At this stage, we're not looking for critical thinking, but simply for students to process the new information you've just introduced, make additional connections, and fill in any gaps. (p. 22)

If teachers are going to "press" with lectures, videos, long explanations, or an in-class reading assignment, they should provide "release" for students in the form of an opportunity for reflection, a bit of journal writing, or conversations in standing pairs.

Talking new information over with a partner reminds students that others may see things differently. One of the two partners in a standing pair share may have a better grasp of what they just heard. Both partners may have questions that can be brought up in a whole-class debriefing following the pair share. Just being able to stand and move following ten minutes of lecture is a plus. Wrestling with the new information can be done in a think, write, pair, share format; students have some time to think about what they just heard, then write it down in a journal. They can then take the journal with them when they pair with a partner (or partners). The last step is a whole-class debrief, where students can share thoughts and questions.

My experience is that students are in a much better frame of mind to share in a whole-class setting if they first have the opportunity to think about it, write about it, talk with a classmate about it, and surface questions that will help clarify their understanding of the information. I have watched as teachers show a short video, then say, "So what do you think?" Students are being asked to share something in public (in front of twenty-eight classmates) before they have had a chance to think about or talk about that something. Needless to say, responses are few (or nonexistent) when students are asked to contribute what they understand *before they understand it themselves.*

The idea is that students need time to digest new information, and letting them talk about it with another student is less frightening than looking for an immediate response. When a short period of lecture (press) is followed by a chance to move, pair, and share (release), students are much more likely to engage in the processing of something to which they were just introduced for the first time.

Build a Better Classroom with Press and Release

Here are a few examples of how the release mechanism can be utilized to increase student engagement in their own learning process.

- If students have four permanent learning partners (for example, Robin, Blue Jay, Sparrow, and Cardinal partners), teachers can quickly move students into discussion mode. When students meet with those partners frequently, they learn the names quickly.

- Consider using a thirty-second piece of music from an upbeat song to send them from their seats to a standing pair share, then back again. If they have permanent partners, you can tell them to "Wave at your Robin partner." Then, "When the music starts, stand with your Robin partner somewhere in the classroom, then face me."

- You might want to talk with your students about the concepts of working and long-term memory. Knowing how the brain

CHAPTER 13

works, and what role each part of the brain plays in the thinking process, helps students understand the whole press-and-release concept.

- Consider talking with a colleague about how he or she uses press and release. A faculty meeting could be devoted to teachers sharing how they use the concept in their classrooms. Over the years, I have seen teachers at all levels use press and release effectively; those uses are out there in the building or the district, waiting to be shared.

CHAPTER 14
KIDS GOTTA MOVE

Every teacher, no matter his or her level of experience in the profession, is a veteran student with countless classroom hours under his or her belt from kindergarten through college. With the exception of Physical Education and wood shop, my experiences in my classrooms as a student led to one salient conclusion: Someone, somewhere was making a fortune selling student desks to the powers that be in every district in the country. Held up by those sturdy pieces of furniture, we became the Sultans of Sitting; no doubt "Ronnie has good posture, whatever his other talents!" made its way onto one of my early report cards (well, perhaps not). Something called the restroom pass became a coveted and much-polished piece of wood that, in some classrooms, was passed from student to student in a way reminiscent of a relay baton in a track meet. Our teachers, who got to move a good deal during the class period, expended much energy telling us not to fidget. The irony did not escape us as we thought of ways to, well, escape.

No one in Emily Konrad's third-grade Iowa classroom thinks of escaping. Konrad, who teaches at Lovejoy Elementary in Des Moines, employs flexible seating. Students decide where they want to sit, with a choice of seating that includes exercise balls, wobble stools, cushions, and myriad other options. Twenge (2017) writes that iGen'ers value choice, and flexible seating goes a long way toward taking care of the fidgets.

Collaborative learning is the norm in Konrad's classroom, and students work together to meet learning targets. While students are elsewhere in the building, she often tapes "task cards" on the walls of her classroom. On their return, students work in pairs to locate a task card, read and analyze the information, discuss a plan to solve the problem,

CHAPTER 14

and then solve it individually and compare their work. If some coaching is in order when it comes to the process, the students understand how to accomplish that. Having completed a task, the pair then moves on to another task card with another problem to process, analyze, and solve. During this activity, Konrad's students are in constant motion as they work together. Konrad's job is to observe, listen, take a few mental notes, and discover where students may be having problems. Activities like this help inform her instructional practice.

While working in groups, Konrad's students also understand that other groups may run into problems, at which point students may visit with colleagues to offer some help. "Students know," says Konrad, "that coaching means guiding or leading, not just giving the answer" (personal communication, April 18, 2019). The combination of flexible seating, frequent changing of collaborative partners, along with the ability to move to check resources or check in with other groups when necessary leads not only to more progress on the part of her students, but to greater satisfaction with the physical learning environment. Konrad has turned movement and choice into two powerful learning tools.

Not everyone has access to the kind of flexible seating arrangements available in Emily Konrad's classroom. However, traditional desks and chairs can be configured so that students can collaborate in small groups, and open spaces can be made available for movement. Here are some ways teachers can harness movement as a learning tool in a traditional classroom setting:

- After a short lecture or video, students can be instructed to stand in pairs somewhere in the classroom to process the new information just imparted.

- Before you ask if there are questions about something students read, heard, or saw, pair them up and ask them to share questions they may have with a single partner. (This is less imposing than sharing with the whole group without a chance to think about what questions one may have.)

- Students can, with some upbeat music playing in the background, stand and move to different locations to obtain whatever materials they may need for the next activity.

- Students, working in pairs or small groups, can move from chart to chart or station to station in what is called a gallery walk (or a walkabout). (Math students, for example, could move from chart to chart as they work on math problems.)

McTighe and Willis (2019) "recommend building in brain breaks, or 'syn-*naps*.' As a regular part of classroom instruction. Syn-*naps* are planned shifts in a learning activity that serve to return the amygdala from overdrive into the optimal state for successful flow of information" (p. 143). The authors point to stretching, moving elsewhere in the classroom, doing exercises, singing songs, and interacting with classmates as necessary.

Build a Better Classroom with Movement

Students today spend many hours per day staring at and manipulating screens of various sizes, and in too many cases this replaces the time we spent outside when I was a kid. "In today's technology-driven, plasma-screened-in world," says Ratey (2008), "it's easy to forget that we are born movers—animals, in fact—because we've engineered movement right out of our lives" (cited in Nash, 2010, p. 5). Teachers can engineer movement into their lesson plans no matter the furniture arrangement in their classrooms. Students will appreciate being able to move, discuss something in pairs, collaborate in groups, and otherwise free themselves from their desks.

Movement can serve as a topic in any faculty meeting, as teachers share with each other and with the whole faculty ways to get students up, moving, pairing, and sharing. Teachers in the same hallway for years can discover, perhaps for the first time, what colleagues are doing when it comes to this important topic.

CHAPTER 14

Here are three important questions when contemplating movement in the classroom:

- Is your classroom configured for movement?
- If not, how can the furniture be rearranged to accommodate movement?
- How can you work movement into your lesson plans?

CHAPTER 15
PERMA PAIRS

For as long as humans have inhabited our planet, affirm Zwiers and Crawford (2011), "conversations have been powerful teachers. They engage, activate, and challenge. They help us build ideas, solve problems, and communicate our thoughts." And in an educational environment where students are always encountering new information, "Conversations strengthen our comprehension of new ideas" (p. 1). But students are sometimes reluctant to test their own ideas and musings in front of a room full of classmates. For students (and for adults, I have found), discussing content-related information with a peer is a lot less intimidating than the prospect of sharing one's thoughts in a large-group setting. Students who feel decidedly uncomfortable sharing information, ideas, or questions with thirty classmates may find a paired conversation much less unnerving.

Face-to-face conversations are important, then, and there are times when teachers may want to quickly put students in pairs so they can discuss something they just saw, heard, or read. This can be accomplished much more quickly and efficiently if students already have permanent partners selected by the students themselves early in the year. They'll pair up with everyone in the class eventually, but if a teacher wants to put students in standing pairs quickly, it is best if they have *permanent partners* with whom they feel comfortable no matter the subject.

Students can choose appointment-clock partners with whom they can then meet regularly (12:00, 3:00, 6:00, and 9:00 partners). They can choose feathered-friends partners (Robin, Blue Jay, Cardinal, Sparrow). One Virginia high school teacher had his students choose ACC partners (University of Virginia, Duke, North Carolina, and North Carolina

CHAPTER 15

State). These perma partners can be chosen by the students during the first week of school, and my experience is that if the teacher has students share frequently, it won't be long before they have memorized their four partners and have gotten to know them well.

Knowing she wants her students to work in pairs and quartets throughout the year, E. C. Glass High School math teacher Mary Marshall begins with icebreakers on the first day of class, so that her students "will feel comfortable answering questions and sharing throughout the rest of the year." Using a beach ball with questions written on it, Marshall has students read a question and answer out loud, then toss the ball to a classmate. "After several questions, the students get to know things about the others in class and realize they have something in common." Later in the year, Marshall can have them pair up quickly with "elbow partners," "quadrant partners," or "solar/lunar partners" so they can share with a single classmate in a way that makes them feel less anxious than in a whole-class setting (personal communication, April 15, 2019).

Build a Better Classroom with Perma Partners

Here are a few situations where paired discussions will help students share their understanding with a partner and raise questions for a later whole-class discussion. They can pair with perma partners:

- to brainstorm listening skills necessary for paired conversations,
- as a way of sharing what they think they know about a subject at the beginning of a unit,
- immediately following a short video clip,
- after reading a short passage,
- after writing for a couple of minutes in a reflective log,
- as a way of surfacing questions at the end of a class period,
- as a way of allowing students to work in pairs on difficult questions,

- following the introduction of new information in lecture format, or

- while working in pairs to interpret a graph, chart, picture, or political cartoon.

If students have been seated for a few minutes, I recommend *standing* pairs, just to get them up and moving. Movement is a powerful learning tool, as we saw in chapter 14. Just standing sends more blood to the brain, carrying with it oxygen and glucose (for energy). I have observed the body language of students forced to sit for more than a few minutes (sometimes for a whole-class period or block!), and it clearly conveys this message: *I need to get up and move*! If each of them has four perma partners with whom they can share at any time, things will go much more smoothly. Confusion is the enemy when it comes to directions; clarity and the comfort of a familiar routine is a teacher's friend.

Keep in mind that on any given day, students will be absent. As students move to meet with their partners, look for the orphans; if there are two, pair them up. If there is one, tell him a trio is perfectly fine, and ask others to adopt that student for the conversation.

Finally, before you have students work in pairs or in groups, spend a good deal of time on listening skills (chapter 11). Listening is the key to successful pairing and group work, and listening and observing students involved in collaborative activities allows teachers to understand where those students are in their progress toward learning targets.

CHAPTER 16
CHOOSING PARTNERS

If students have perma partners, as we saw in the last chapter, teachers can, at any time, call on everyone to stand, move, and meet with his or her 9:00 partner, Cardinal partner, or whomever. Obviously, teachers won't want to limit paired conversations to only four partners. The best biology teacher I ever met had his students pairing for discussions with everyone in the room at least once by the end of the first week of school. This is a great way to learn names quickly on the way to building working relationships in classrooms.

My experience over the years is that teachers are often at a loss as to how to choose—or have students choose—classroom partners for an activity or project. I have seen teachers give this instruction: "Okay, everyone. Stand, choose a partner for the next activity, and move with your partner somewhere in the room!" And then Murphy's Law (anything that can go wrong will go wrong) takes over. Students look around the room, searching for a best friend, then get upset when someone else pairs up with that person. Confusion reigns and the teacher expresses frustration—and often blames the students. Teachers who experience this more than once often simply give up on paired activities unless they have carefully chosen the partners themselves. But there are plenty of options available to avoid chaos and disappointment on the part of students and teachers.

I'm guessing the number of ways to choose pairs in a classroom is limitless, but here are a few:

- I walked into a fifth-grade classroom after lunch. The teacher was there, but the students had not yet arrived. Listed on the whiteboard were student pairs. The students looked at the

CHAPTER 16

board, paired, grabbed the bag full of materials for the task at hand, and went anywhere in the room they could find space. Instructions for the actual activity followed, but the pairing was already done, along with the gathering of necessary materials. While those fifth graders did not choose their partners in this case, they had plenty of choices as to where they could work together in the room. Some were on the floor, while others sat next to each other at tables.

- Kathy Galford, when she taught sixth-grade language arts at Greenbrier Middle School (VA), often had students choose random pairs by cutting playing cards in half and distributing them throughout the room so that they were on the students' desks when they arrived. All they had to do when she gave the word to move was to find the person with the other half of that card, then stand facing Galford, waiting for instructions.

- In an elementary school classroom, the teacher distributed geometric shapes to the desks of students before they entered the classroom in the morning. When she wanted to begin the paired activity, she simply had them stand, grab their cards, and pair up with the person who had the same shape.

- In another classroom, the teacher placed the beginning of a complete sentence on half of the cards, with the most likely sentence completion for each of those stems on other cards. Students had to complete the sentences, and that resulted in random pairs for the afternoon.

- In one high school classroom, and I often use this pairing strategy, students were instructed to stand and move to an open area in the classroom. The teacher then told them to raise their right hands high, take two or three steps in any direction, shake hands with a new partner, and then turn and face her in these newly chosen pairs.

- In an elementary classroom, students had cards on their desks, each with a simple math problem or, for half the class, the answers. Students stood with the cards and were instructed to find their partners by correctly matching the problem (42 + 12 =) with the answer (54).

- In Joy White's fifth-grade classroom at Mountain View Elementary (VA), her day begins with morning meetings built around a theme. Her students begin in a class circle, but they often meet in small groups. In the latter case, relates White, "they push in their chairs and move to the music around the room. When the music stops, they find a chair closest to them at a table, and that's who they share with that day" (personal communication, April 19, 2019).

Build a Better Classroom with Multiple Pairing Techniques

There are any number of ways partners can be chosen, and I encourage teachers to be creative in their approach. Ask teachers who regularly create pairs for standing pair shares or other activities how they accomplish it without confusion. The brain loves novelty. Importantly, the exercise involved in moving about the room shifts more oxygen into the brains of students who may have been sitting for a while: "To improve your thinking skills," says Medina (2014), "move" (p. 35).

Sixth-grade English teacher Kathy Galford used this pairing technique often: "When cued to find a partner (when the music starts), [her students] knew to walk towards the middle of the room, and once they found their partner, the pairs moved towards the perimeter of the room" (personal communication, March 27, 2019). The center of the room, crowded at first, quickly emptied as partners were chosen and pairs formed. The most important thing Galford did was to have them practice this until they got it down. Each of her many transition processes was practiced by her students until she was satisfied with the results. Because time is of the essence in classrooms, transitions often need to be accomplished quickly. But they also need to be done smoothly and efficiently.

Here are a few tips when students are choosing partners:

- Those involved in real estate talk about location, location, location. For teachers at every grade level, the analogy is practice,

CHAPTER 16

practice, practice. In every case above, what those teachers did worked because they practiced the pairing techniques until they became routine.

- Once students are in standing pairs, it is a simple matter to move them into standing quartets: "Standing near you and your partner is another pair of students. When the music starts, make a quartet with that pair." If pairs are needed once again, the pairs can break off easily, ready to go.

- Music can accompany the pairing process, and I suggest a time limit be established upfront. Some teachers use a timer. When practicing getting into standing pairs early in the year, make sure that students don't gradually push the time limit. If they don't get it right, do it again until they do, and keep doing it until it becomes routine.

Remember, getting students into pairs is not the main event. I have seen teachers take too much time using pairing techniques that waste time. Efficiency and speed are essential because there is always much to do related to the learning process; pairing constitutes a starting point for activities that require paired collaboration (a short discussion about a reading passage or short video students have just seen, a conversation about a reflective journal entry students have completed, coming up with a short list of questions students may have before moving on, brainstorming in pairs before doing so in a whole-class setting, practicing speaking and listening skills, to name a few).

CHAPTER 17

PRIMING

Growing up along Lake Erie in the 1950s and 1960s, several of us would often sit outside a friend's cottage and chat about topics of interest to teenagers, a conversation that might have included which Beatles song just hit number one on the charts, or which pitcher in last night's game "had his stuff." Remove the discussion du jour, and the only sound was the breaking of some gentle waves on the shore, accompanied by a few crickets discussing matters of interest to them. Take away the conversations of teenagers and crickets, and the silence would have matched that of my history classroom when I asked, "Who knows the answer to this question?" Even the crickets, had they been present in room 205, might have hesitated to reply.

The problem with that or any other content-related query aimed in the general direction of my eighth graders was that I expected an answer before anyone had time to think about the question. This was not the first rodeo for these veteran scholars, and Eddie knew that any answers on offer from his classmates would come from my fan club in the first row. He could look suitably puzzled, then take a close look at his notes, such as they were. The game I was playing included only a few participants; the rest, including Eddie, were spectators.

When students have taken a page or two of notes while listening to the teacher lecture, they can be forgiven if they don't have total recall of what they just heard or wrote. Allowing them to stand—notebooks and pen in hand—and share what they wrote with a classmate, they will no doubt discover that each of them missed something or has a question about something else. They can also write down something they don't understand, or perhaps one of the partners can clear up misconceptions without asking questions to the teacher. Asking questions immediately after students are done writing does not allow them to absorb the information; talking about what they heard and wrote with a partner helps with understanding and might even surface misunderstandings or questions that only the teacher can answer at that moment.

If we want students to wrestle with and attempt to understand new information, they need to talk about it. The only way to get everyone involved is to get everyone involved. This is where Kagan's (1994) "simultaneity principle" comes in. In a classroom with thirty students, there can be fifteen simultaneous conversations going on. The teacher's role at that point is to walk around the room, eavesdropping in a subtle way on the various discussions. When she hears a particularly interesting point being made, she can ask that student if he or she will share it later on. If the teacher does that with four or five students, all she has to do is remember four or five names for the whole-class discussion that will follow the standing pair shares.

Eddie can hide in a classroom full of his peers; he can't hide in a pair. Each partner in a pair is responsible for the other person. I have been in classrooms at every grade level where students are asked to explain something to a partner, ask questions or paraphrase to provide clarity. Listening becomes as important, if not more so, than speaking. Everyone in the room is either listening or speaking, and everyone is thinking. Talking is thinking, and thinking is learning.

Teachers have a choice: They can do most of the talking (and most of the thinking), or they can increase the number of conversations and the quality of the thinking going on. For students who have been sitting for a while, listening to a short lecture or watching a video clip, need to get up and move anyway, so why not pair everyone up and get them engaged in face-to-face dialogue. This can be followed by a whole-class discussion where far more answers are now available should the teacher choose to ask a few questions. This is called priming, and the analogy is that of the priming of a pump before bringing it into full operation.

Build a Better Classroom with Priming

When students are working in groups, involved in a project, and invested in the conversations they are having, teachers will often say,

PRIMING

"Look this way, please." The problem with this is that their minds may be on what they are doing at that moment; they may not even register the teacher's four-word command. Allen (2002) tells us that "It may be more useful to the students in this situation to prime them by announcing 'You have thirty seconds more. Please try to bring your conversations to a close within that time'" (p. 103). This gives groups time to wrap up the conversations and put an imaginary bookmark in the proceedings. They are in a better position at that point to return to their work later.

While listening to paired conversations, you might ask one or both partners in a pair to share something you overheard during the debrief. Have them decide who will share, then *don't forget to call on them*. Also, don't force them to share; if they say they would rather not, say, "That's fine. Maybe some other time." This primes them by letting them know in advance that one of them will be asked to share something they talked about. It also gives them time, if they wish, to decide which partner will do the sharing and what he or she will say.

Finally, near the end of the period, and after some intensive work on content, the teacher can take a few minutes to ask for questions they might have. The questions can then be charted for later use or as the homework for that night: "Pick one of these questions we have charted on the whiteboard (it could be your question or someone else's) and research it tonight. Return tomorrow with some possible answers."

The point here is that students can learn from each other by talking with partners *before* the teacher asks questions or asks *for* questions. They can share whatever questions they may have with a partner. Priming takes time, but produces results.

CHAPTER 18
WHOLE-CLASS DISCUSSIONS

Like all humans, teachers feel comfortable in routines that have been repeated so often they are second nature. And like all humans, teachers feel uneasy with—and often frightened of—change. Tradition in our educational system requires teachers as talkers and students as listeners—or at least *pretend* listeners. If teachers today, as was the case with me for most of my teaching career, are into compliance and control, rather than actual student growth and learning, opening a classroom of thirty-two ninth graders to a discussion dealing with the U.S. Constitution's Separation of Powers may seem like a sure invitation to student rebellion and ultimate chaos. "Many teachers," affirm Walsh and Sattes (2015), "are uncomfortable with their departure from their traditional role, in which the teacher controls who speaks, speaks before and after each student, speaks primarily in questions, and reacts to every student answer by evaluating its value or correctness" (p. 35). Again, if this is familiar to teachers who inhabited many a traditional classroom setting, it is because the tradition of a teacher-centered, compliance-and-control classroom runs deep in our culture.

In observing classrooms over many years, one conclusion I have drawn is that whole-class conversations are far more interesting, valuable, and successful when students have not only read about a topic, but have written and talked about it as well. We don't just want students to feel comfortable with the topic at hand; we want them to feel comfortable with *discussing* it in front of their peers. For students who are as mired in tradition as their teachers, offering an opinion on something may seem a bridge too far. Allowing them to discuss the topic in standing pairs (Priming, chapter 17) gives them the opportunity to road-test their thoughts,

CHAPTER 18

opinions, evidence, and/or conclusions. The more confident students become at verbalizing their thoughts in pairs, the more confidence they will display in whole-class settings.

When students move from standing pairs back to their seats for a whole-class discussion, they have broached the subject, talked about it, and raised some questions. Teachers who have been listening to the paired discussions can prime the pump further by asking if Melanie is willing to share what she and Sid talked about as partners. Once Melanie begins the conversation, others may be encouraged to follow.

> "Brad and I were talking about this idea, and we agreed . . ."
> "I hadn't thought about this point until Marcy mentioned it a few minutes ago in our discussion."

The teacher's role in all this begins with an issue that is "sufficiently relevant and provocative to engage students emotionally" (Walsh and Sattes, 2015, p. 18). The teacher can then frame a question that will get the ball rolling, but she cannot assume things will run smoothly after that. This is where process facilitation skills come in. Her job at that point is, according to Walsh and Sattes, to "(1) listen to understand; (2) scaffold with statements, questions, or other appropriate moves; and (3) monitor to ensure equitable participation" (p. 76). Also, to keep things moving, teachers who might normally provide evaluative comments need to back off and let students talk.

There are many things (verbal and nonverbal) that teachers can use to keep the conversational ball in play. Speakers are always encouraged by a nod of the head or a quick statement of encouragement ("I see." or "Yes."). These working responses say, "I'm listening and I want to hear more." Remember, when students are in pairs, the listener is quite likely to mimic the gestures and verbal phrases and statements used by the teacher. This sends the clear message that listening is an important part of any paired or group conversation.

In chapters 11 and 12, I highlighted the importance of silence in the thinking process. In any paired, small-group, or whole-class conversation, wait time becomes important. Teachers tend not to like silence; we want *someone* to say *something*, and quickly. It is worth the time, however, to allow for pauses after a question is asked or answered, or immediately following a bit of sharing on the part of a student. This pause gives everyone time to reflect on what was just said. It also gives students a moment to decide whether or not they want to piggyback on that last point or come up with a possible answer to a question a classmate just posed.

Here is one of those big little things that can waste time and cause confusion: Students need to learn to express themselves confidently and loudly enough to be heard and understood in a classroom full of peers. Over and over again, I see teachers ask a question, only to have a student speak so softly in reply that only the teacher can hear him or her, at which point the teacher has to repeat what was said. Avoid the temptation to become a walking amplifier! Train your students to speak up and speak in an articulate fashion. Repeating what students say wastes valuable time, and speaking into one's textbook or desk does nothing to build speaking skills clearly set forth in the speaking and listening skills section of the Common Core or in the language arts skills of state standards.

I have seen substantial, well-facilitated whole-class conversations in classrooms; I have also seen discussions that died quick deaths or got out of hand because the teacher did not exercise his or her role as facilitator of the process. Making these interactions work requires patience and skill, and most of all, it takes a teacher willing to take risks on behalf of kids.

Build a Better Classroom with Whole-Class Discussions

One of the best college instructors I had while pursuing my teaching degree was a philosophy professor who made it a point to get everyone involved in whole-class discussions of material we had just read. He asked guiding questions and kept us engaged in a way that made me look forward to *participating* in his class. Unlike most of my other classes, we were not *attendees*; he made sure we participated, and we soon understood that we needed to be ready for that class by having done the required reading or research.

Having observed a great many whole-class discussions over the past seventeen years, I have concluded that it is essential that teachers ask open-ended questions that allow students to share ideas without thinking the teacher is on the hunt for that one right answer. Conversations are valuable because they allow us to share ideas in an atmosphere free of the kinds of judgments that can bring the whole discussion to an abrupt—and decidedly uncomfortable or embarrassing—halt.

"When leading the discussion," Gunter, Estes, and Schwab (2003) suggest that teachers "frequently ask follow-up questions that force students to reason aloud, to air their work so to speak." Further, "The tone of your probing should encourage: Tell me what you think? Why do you think so?" (p. 187). Teachers can also ask students to expand on, explain, develop further, or rephrase an idea they have contributed to the conversation. Teachers can also pull others into the conversation: "Amber, what do you think?" (p. 187).

Finally, conversations, in pairs or groups, according to Zwiers and Crawford (2011), help students build oral language and critical-thinking skills, along with those related to content understanding. And every conversation a student has helps build confidence that will serve them not only in school but also in relationships and in the workplace, where communication skills are valued—and often lacking.

CHAPTER 19

HAVE AT IT!

When I was a kid on Gibson Street, I received for Christmas one year a set of Lincoln Logs, the jumbo set, actually. I'm sure there must have been a set of directions somewhere, but I wasn't interested in directions. I dumped the container out on the floor in front of me and dug in. There were plenty of pictures of buildings that had been constructed out of the logs, and that was enough for me. I just figured it out. When I was done I sat back in satisfaction, took apart the existing edifice, and started over again. Trial and error was my stock in trade as a four- or five-year-old construction magnate. Figuring things out was what I did in those days. I did not spend a lot of time planning. I did spend a great deal of time doing; after all, the fun was in the doing. I committed a good many unforced errors along the way, but that was all part of the deal.

Educators, and I speak from experience here, can plan things into extinction. A district will order up a new program at great expense, then spend an inordinate amount of time getting it ready for prime time. A teacher will put off the implementation of a lesson plan because it isn't quite finished. A student, and I had some experience with this, will wait until that last resource drops into place to start a term paper that is now due in a few days.

Sometimes, we just have to get moving in the right direction; at which point some helpful on-the-job training is warranted. As a yearbook adviser on my second tour of duty, I told a new copywriter to "just start writing" with what she had by way of quotes and background, without perseverating over the accumulation of further notes and interviews. "Had she not started writing, she might well have planned her way right past the submission deadline" (Nash, 2019, p. xix). She had the help of fellow staffers, anchor stories, a set of written standards, and a handy checklist for grammar. And she had me if all else failed, but planning something into extinction or perseverating to the point of inaction was not an option.

One of my favorite authors on leadership, Michael Fullan (2010), cautions leaders not to get too caught up in the planning: "Do not load up on vision, evidence, and sense of urgency," says Fullan (2010). "Rather, give people new experiences in relatively nonthreatening experiences, and build on it" (p. 25). This is why I always suggest to teachers that before they throw students into groups, let them cut their eye teeth on listening skills with many partners in seated and standing pair shares, where they can build on the mistakes and unforced errors they are likely to commit. These early paired conversations are not high-stakes situations as students working in groups will encounter in PBL situations later on. Collaboration begins with communication skill sets best introduced early and in low-stakes efforts on which students can build as they work toward more complex tasks and projects. And, the introduction of those skills can begin on the first day of school.

I don't really have anything against planning, and there is much to be said for a good lesson plan, but the fun is in the doing, not in the planning. A friend and I wrote two mystery stories when we were eleven years old, and I still have the tablets on which we wrote the manuscripts in our number 2 pencils. The tablets are loaded with erasures and sentences that are crossed out. We made our mistakes and we made our corrections, but the enjoyment came in the writing of the stories. It was one of our teachers who encouraged us to keep moving on the project and I sat down at a typewriter in my aunt's office supply store and pecked out the books on mimeograph masters, after which we printed them out, stapled them, and sold them at a store on the corner of Lake Street and Main.

If we as teachers can get students started on the writing, the discussing, and the creating, mistakes can be sorted out along the way. A teacher wandering around the classroom while thirty students take part in fifteen paired discussions can determine which listening skills need mending. The fifth-grade teacher who works the room while students write persuasive essays can not only help students as they write but can figure out where he needs to go next with his instruction related to grammar, sentence construction, and much else.

Both learning and teaching are in the doing, but teachers working with students—and administrators working with teachers—must remove fear of failure from the equation. Fullan (2010) stressed the nonthreatening environment that best serves people trying out something unfamiliar in an area well outside their comfort zone. I have seen teachers unintentionally chase students from outside their comfort zones back into them by making the new experience too painful. Teachers who clearly understand something but can't figure out why a student doesn't get that something right away can express frustration, use sarcasm, and otherwise short-circuit the continuous improvement process for kids who in good faith forged ahead into—for them—uncharted territory.

I love it when I am in a classroom where students are allowed to be students, and teachers allow themselves to be students as well. Learning isn't something we give to kids, and most of the learning is not in the planning. The learning is in the doing, and the best teachers I know dump the Lincoln Logs out on the floor, turn to the kids, and say, "Have at it!"

Building a Better Classroom with a Have-at-It Spirit

It is wonderful observing in classrooms where wide-open, obviously exciting group projects are underway. The level of engagement is high, and teachers can circulate among groups, asking guiding questions, providing a bit of feedback on request. If the project is a multi-day effort, the teacher will often hold a five- or ten-minute debrief at the end of the class period, or they may begin the next day's activities with comments or questions that fit the "have-at-it" project environment. I will often hear questions and comments along these lines:

- "A couple of you posted questions last night concerning this assignment, the answers to which should help everyone."
- "I sensed yesterday that some of you may be worried about making mistakes as you work on this project. Don't be. Mistakes are just learning opportunities, as athletic coaches and company CEOs will tell us. In this room we are all encouraged to make mistakes, using them to guide us as we move forward."

CHAPTER 19

- "Before we get started today, I want to thank Rachel's group for helping me understand something yesterday. Specifically, . . ."
- "Everyone, Marvin has agreed to share something he learned while working on this assignment that I think we could all benefit from. Go ahead, Marvin."

If we want students to "have at it," whatever "it" is, the classroom culture must be one that welcomes—and encourages—mistakes. Unforced errors and missteps when working on a project or an assignment qualify as feedback. Feedback is not right or wrong or good or bad. Feedback is both formative and informative. It helps us *as we learn*. But to make mistakes, kids must take part in the doing. Mistakes are as inevitable as they are useful; ask any coach.

Michael Fullan (2010), in *Motion Leadership*, reminds all of us that "to get anywhere, you have to *do* something" (p. 32). Good advice. Have at it.

CHAPTER 20
PROCESS-RELATED DIPSTICK CHECKS

In my younger days, back in high school, I owned a seafoam green 1961 Chevy. It cost me $80. The dealer threw in a few just-this-side-of-threadbare tires to get me on the road (and, no doubt, out of his office so he could sell a new car for considerably more money). My car used oil at a prodigious rate, and I had to check the oil dipstick every day to gauge how far I could go without digging into the case of oil in our garage and feeding the beast. That dipstick told me what I needed to know. It told me what I needed to do. It didn't take much time to use that dipstick, but it kept my car on the road.

A few days before writing this, I presented to 100+ elementary teachers in a three-hour professional- development workshop in Iowa. After ninety minutes of the session, followed by a short break, I held forth once again. About five minutes into the second half of the workshop, one of the participants turned the back of his notebook in my direction. On the back cover, he had printed the following: MIC. Mic is short for microphone, something I had forgotten to turn back on after the break. Without his timely intervention (he was a band director, by the way), I would have continued on in blissful ignorance, making participants cup their ears and lean over to a neighbor, saying, "What did he say?" No doubt my voice would have suffered as well.

Feedback is, quite simply put, the lifeblood of the continuous improvement process. We ask teachers to change in order to improve what they are doing, and change requires risk. And, as we saw in the last chapter, risk brings with it mistakes, unforced errors, and inevitable failure somewhere along the way. When things happen that make us wonder why we went out on that limb in the first place, the best thing we can do is *not*

CHAPTER 20

to withdraw and refuse to try anything else new, but to find out what went wrong and fix it. Knowing we can fix something makes us more willing to continue to take risks.

Feedback is often not requested but is nevertheless appreciated, as it was for me in Iowa. The value of the dipstick lies in its use by someone who comes to know the value of the information it provides. Teachers are, I have found, often reluctant to look for things that might suggest that the lesson they just facilitated could use some tweaking. Teachers willing to put what they do—and how they do it—under the microscope stand to improve their own performance, along with their students' learning.

Every teacher, I would suspect, and I include myself here, has tried something new in his or her classroom, only to have the proverbial train leave the track at some point in the proceedings. The students who took part in the lesson that day are in a position to provide feedback, if the teacher is willing to ask. Their perspective is different from that of the teacher, and, frankly, most students really want things to run smoothly.

When a teacher has tried something new, the perfect time to seek feedback from the people who most benefit from improvements is right after the lesson or the activity. This can be done anonymously, using sticky notes on which students can offer input. Or the teacher can call a time-out and use a plus/delta (+/△). This can be as simple as two columns on the whiteboard, one with a + at the top of the left-hand column (What went well for you?) and a △ at the top of the right-hand column (What was confusing?). Doing this requires a bit of risk-taking on the part of teachers who have not only never done this, but have never seen it used in a classroom. However, if the use of this feedback tool helps improve that lesson or activity for years to come, it is well worth the effort.

One sixth-grade history teacher gave her students two stickies every Friday, asking them to write down what went well for them during that week on one sticky, along with something she could improve upon on the other. She showed me a whole batch of those sticky notes; the students had learned over time that *she read them*, then made changes based on their feedback—and she let them know how much their input helped *her* help *them*. Looking at and categorizing those dipstick checks took time—on the weekend—but she told me it was well worth it. Also, the quality of the feedback improved once they understood that the whole exercise was legitimate, and not for show.

Another way for teachers to get feedback as far as the process is concerned is to invite a colleague to observe part of a classroom period, perhaps twenty minutes or so. Ask the observer to look for the following by watching not the teacher, but the students:

- While I was giving verbal instructions for this activity, did students seem to be confused?
- I left the written directions on the screen as they worked. Did you notice if anyone looked at them as their group worked?
- As students worked in groups during this activity, did their body language demonstrate that they understood what was required, or were they unsure about what to do?
- Were students engaged, or did they seem disconnected from the activity?

If you have someone visit your classroom, don't overload that willing observer. Give them a very few key questions; keep it simple. Meet with that colleague and limit the amount of time you take from them to debrief. If you say you will take fifteen minutes, take fifteen minutes. Take a few notes, then take the time to reflect on what he or she said. Combine that with what the kids contributed by way of feedback, make necessary changes, and commit to the improved processes next time through.

Build a Better Classroom with Dipstick Checks

I used to wait until the last day of school to get feedback from my students in the form of a four-page feedback booklet. I learned a great deal from that document, and it may have helped me during the next school year, but what I gleaned from it was simply too late to help the 140+ students who had spent the previous 4 9-week grading periods with me. A periodic dipstick check would have informed my instruction by improving my processes, and that would have benefited my students in real time.

Classroom processes are interchangeable; changes that improve one lesson can be used with another. If a colleague observes that you are speaking too quickly when you give directions for one activity, the

CHAPTER 20

subsequent changes will positively affect every subsequent set of directions. If students are confused by the written directions for a project, their feedback can be valuable in making the next set of directions clear and unambiguous. Most students are in the teacher's corner, especially if they know he or she values their opinions and solicits their feedback. They will do what they can to keep the process train on the track. Periodic dipstick checks can assist those important processes; my guess is that in the future everyone in that community of learners, including the learner-in-chief, will benefit from version 2.0. As with my 1961 Chevy, periodic dipstick checks are necessary to keep things running smoothly.

Mistakes are also necessary components of the continuous improvement process, and as one North Carolina principal told his teachers constantly: *Go out on a limb. If it breaks off, pick yourself up, dust yourself off, and find a new limb.*

CHAPTER 21
REFLECTIVE LEARNERS

At the break during a presentation at a high school, an English teacher asked for my advice concerning the grading of her term paper assignments. She lamented the fact that she spent hours each evening going over the rough drafts, with the final product due a few days hence. She then repeated the process in summative fashion, using a red pen to record gobs of comments, leaving room at the top of the first page for a grade. She admitted to drinking gallons of coffee and staying up well into the wee hours in order to memorialize her feedback in written form.

I asked her if she ever had her students exchange drafts and provide formative feedback for each other, and she said it was her job to provide feedback, a job that was apparently driving her to distraction, and to the kitchen for bottomless cups of coffee. A teacher who insists on serving as the sole source of feedback for more than a hundred students may well wonder on occasion why she didn't take that sales job with cousin Brenda.

As a yearbook adviser, I had my copywriters work as proofreaders for each other, and that was certainly helpful. They did what I did when going over a piece of copy with a staffer; the draft, the pencil, and the eraser stayed with the one who had written the copy as they discussed strengths and possible improvements. Hattie and Clarke (2019) take this a step further, suggesting that the student responsible for the work read it out loud for the partner. "When the author reads their work out loud pen in hand, they see their errors immediately." Also, "Students have more natural conversations, interrupting each other or asking for clarification and so on, than when they are in a dialogue with a teacher" (p. 107). They

CHAPTER 21

are just flat-out more comfortable discussing their work with a peer than with an adult.

This does not mean, however, that teachers should not "work the room" while individuals or groups wrestle with tasks or larger, more complex projects. Teacher/student conferences serve as relationship builders, and, write Stiggins and Chappuis (2012), "permits individualization that works very well when students are at different levels of achievement, such as in the development of their math or writing proficiencies" (p. 273). I have observed many classroom teachers at all levels "hunker down" next to a student and provide excellent feedback, while asking guiding questions that allow students to reflect on their own work during the conversation.

Here are some advantages of teacher/student conferences over written feedback:

- The student has the opportunity—right then—to ask questions and receive immediate answers.

- By opening with something personal, the teacher can further develop important teacher/student relationships over the course of many stops during that class period.

- The teacher can ask the student to read something aloud. This allows the student to hear their own work, not just read it.

- A teacher can take that [private] opportunity to offer some praise to the student, something that might have caused great embarrassment in front of the class.

- The teacher can ask questions like, "How can this sentence be improved?" or "Is there another descriptor that might be used here?"

- Finally, affirm Stiggins and Chappuis (2012), "students can describe what is and is not working for them" (p. 273). Feelings like this are not obvious in written work, so several drafts can go back and forth without surfacing obstacles or other bumps in the road that can be brought into the open during a one-on-one conversation. Multiple conversations between teachers and students prior to the submission of the final draft or project allow students to make periodic adjustments before that final draft or project is pending.

I can remember getting the rough draft of a high school term paper back, just days before the final paper was due. It was bleeding red ink, as I recall, and there was much to do, much to change, and much to fix, prior to submission. I don't remember if I got depressed looking at all the mistakes and unforced errors on my part, along with a multitude of comments and suggestions on her part, or if I took it all in stride. No doubt as I strode out of the classroom that day, I knew what I would be doing that weekend.

Feedback does not have to come in a torrent; it can come in small bites when students seek the help of peers, when teachers keep their comments to a precious few at different stages of a student project, when teachers make frequent trips to student desks or to groups working at tables, or when the teacher asks the musical question, "What is the next step for you?"

Going back to the English teacher who was up every night with a box of red pens and lots of caffeine, that all-important last draft can benefit from multiple sources of feedback. Feedback can—and should—come in bits and bytes over a period of time, allowing students to make a change here and an adjustment there on the continuous improvement highway.

Build a Better Classroom by Providing Time to Let Learners Learn

One of the things that characterized my early classrooms was that I allowed no time to reflect on new information, and I neglected to let students spend time with old information. I was in a hurry, and this did not allow time for students to be students; I created rooms full of notetakers and pretend listeners. Time should be built into the daily schedule for students to self-assess their work and come to grips with their mistakes. We need to help them understand that there is nothing wrong with making mistakes, and that they serve a purpose in helping us get better at whatever it is we seek to do. Teachers who finally conclude that they are not the only teachers in the room are, I have found, happier campers.

CHAPTER 21

Sometimes less is more; time can be built into the daily routine for personal reflection, peer feedback, and questions students are not afraid to ask. And some of those questions can be asked of classmates.

In Katie White's *Softening the Edges: Assessment Practices That Honor K-12 Teachers and Learners* (2017), the author encourages teachers to build classroom cultures based on trust, risk-taking, and optimism:

> We need to create classrooms where there is time for reinforcement and practice and where everything is not always new. Moving too quickly with minimal attention to retention and application stifles a learner's ability to be reflective. In these instances, students may stop caring about what others think about the few choices they actually get to make, and they certainly won't take the time to consider how they, themselves, feel about their learning. (p. 130)

Teachers can—and should—make decisions about how they and their students spend their time in classrooms. Self-assessment is an important part of the learning process, and it should not be confused, says White, with evaluation. As my yearbook staffers worked independently and interdependently on layouts, photography, and written copy, there was no grade. All of what we did was done after school, which took the pressure off as far as grades go. All I wanted them to do was to improve from layout to layout, and from story to story. We worked against a set of national standards for yearbooks, and feedback came in many forms—and it was all formative in nature.

Learning involves reflection and the seeking of help from many sources, most often in small bites that can be digested easily and effectively. In classrooms where collaboration is the norm, feedback is available immediately from fellow teammates, peers in other groups, anchor products (like the award-winning yearbooks we collected and devoured), notes, textbooks, and myriad other resources. "Students need time," says White (2017), "to reflect, time to experiment, time to practice, and time to refine" (p. 130). If we move too quickly through a curriculum or textbook, there is no time to do these things. This means there is no time to learn, and no time to let learners *be* learners.

CHAPTER 22
PURPOSEFUL AND THOUGHTFUL PRAISE

At the beginning of my freshman year in high school, I worked in a supermarket in my hometown. Other than delivering newspapers for a couple of years in junior high school, this was my first job, and I was determined to make the most of it. I started out bagging groceries; there were times on a Saturday or Sunday when business at the registers was relatively slow. During those occasional downtimes, I would grab a push broom or a scrub brush and clean the floor, shelving, or anything else that needed cleaning. I chose to be perpetually busy; I wanted to contribute.

Paul, the owner/manager of the store, hunkered down next to me one day while I was scrubbing the kick plate under a produce case, something no one had asked me to do. He told me how much he appreciated my efforts on behalf of the store's efficient and effective operation. He told me the kick plates that were getting my attention needed it badly. And he gave me a nickel-an-hour raise, which in the early 1960s was much appreciated on my part. But it was the fact that he noticed, appreciated, and acknowledged (privately) my efforts that meant the most. Had he ambled by, saying, "Great job, Ron!" it wouldn't have meant as much to me. He took the time to get down next to me and acknowledge my time on the extra mile, with some specific praise—and a raise in pay I had not requested.

Mike Gershon (2018) makes the point that praise in the classroom needs to be specific, and that students will spot praise that is not genuine in a nanosecond. I have made the point many times that for veteran students this is not their first rodeo. They know empty platitudes when they hear them, and they spot praise that is not genuine. "To deliver

CHAPTER 22

genuine praise, you need to look at what students are doing and think about how one or more elements of this are good" (p. 69). And Gershon says teachers need to provide truly genuine and specific praise regularly.

Bits of what I call throwaway praise don't accomplish anything, except sending the student the message that the teacher may not have read what the student wrote. Writing "Great job!" on one of my students' homework assignments told them nothing, and not helped or guided them at all. A classroom full of sophomores who hear their teacher frequently use stock phrases like, "Excellent work!" or "Well done!" can be excused for discounting such seemingly insincere praise. If students think that the teacher uses these phrases only to make them feel good, then these throwaway lines become worthless.

Gershon (2018) provides two examples of praise:

(1) Wonderful work today, Yolande, you are doing great.

(2) Wonderful work today, Yolande, you kept going even when things were challenging. That's what we want to see. (p. 69)

The first example lacks specificity. The second refers "to something real and tangible which happened during the lesson" (p. 69).

Specific praise is great as far as it goes, but it is not feedback. "Unlike feedback," write Frey, Fisher, and Smith (2019), "praise doesn't give a student any direction as to what to do next, or any information about why something he or she did was successful" (p. 24). Feedback is the lifeblood of the continuous improvement process, but teachers should not overlook the value of specific and genuine praise. I recommend that teachers keep their praise private; some students—and many adults—don't like or appreciate public praise.

Hattie and Clarke (2019) point out that praise that is given too often, and that is unrelated to performance, can turn students into praise junkies. Praise, say the authors, "can undermine resilience, as it sends messages that it is the student rather than their involvement and persistence in learning that determines success." Praise junkies "seek positive commendations to confirm their self-esteem and look acceptable in front of their peers" (p. 43). The authors go on to say that this kind of frequent and misguided praise can often keep students from taking the kinds of risks that may bring mistakes and failure; better to play it safe.

There is something else I have noticed from my place in the balcony as I observe classrooms at all grade levels: When a teacher goes overboard with public praise for one student, it sets the standard for subsequent offerings of such praise. When teachers use superlatives like "Fantastic!" or "Give me a high five, Eddie!" with the volume turned up, others in the room come to expect the same treatment. This is why specific, performance- or content-related feedback given quietly and without fanfare is more valuable to students, and less likely to cause problems. A superlative that comes privately at the end of a useful bit of feedback, as was the case with my boss at the supermarket, carries more weight.

Building a Better Classroom with Thoughtful Praise

Here are a few hints related to the use of praise:

- Avoid using too much praise. I knew someone who walked around saying, "Good job!" to nearly everyone in the room. It meant little, and it became as annoying as it was worthless. Consider the praise that you employ in your classroom as a matter of course. Is it generally specific in nature, or could it be construed by students as insincere? (Remember, sincerity is in the ears of the beholder.)

- Tie your praise to specific feedback: "Your use of verb subject agreement has improved over the past few weeks. Well done." The praise follows the feedback. "Well done!" on its own tells the student nothing useful.

- If you are gathering information about students on index cards during the first week of school, perhaps one of the questions could be: If praise is warranted, do you prefer that it is public or private? (A former director of our department in central office asked that question to all of us, then followed through based on our input. We appreciated it.)

CHAPTER 22

- I once had a teacher call me to the front of the classroom to tell me that my writing was improving over time, and she gave me specific examples of how that was so. I have not forgotten that conversation, and it took place fifty-seven years ago. It was thoughtful, specific, and private—just the way I liked it.

CHAPTER 23
THE SMOOTH SHIFTING OF TRANSITIONAL GEARS

I learned to drive a car with a standard shift in my mid-20s, and did so in Western Pennsylvania in an area replete with hills, valleys, and a good deal of snow and ice. When I came to a stop on the often-icy hill heading up to our house in the winter, I had to be mindful of how what I did with the clutch, brake, and gas pedal affected those ahead of me and, as always seemed to be the case, much too close behind me on a steep incline. I had to concentrate on processes unfamiliar to me as I persisted in becoming proficient. I improved with practice, of course, and came to enjoy driving both our cars, neither of which had an automatic shift. I eventually got to the point where friends did not mind riding with me.

A teacher erases the white board while she tells her eighth graders to open their journals. When she turns around to face the class, most of them don't have their journals out, much less open. She gets upset, saying something to the effect of, "Didn't you hear me? I told you to get your journals open?" This is not a good start to the next phase of the lesson.

The fact is that many of the students, perhaps most, did not hear her. Many were talking while she was erasing the board. Also, she was talking to the board, not to the students. She did not have their attention at the moment she gave them her instructions. What she was in the process of erasing was the result of some brainstorming in a whole-class discussion format. Because they were not ready when she turned around, she was upset with them and gave voice to her frustration in a way that did no one any good. The brainstorming activity had been successful, but the upbeat mood created during those twenty minutes or so was ruined because the teacher did not do what was necessary to shift gears smoothly as she had them transition to the next phase of the lesson.

CHAPTER 23

A classroom teacher has scores of such gear-shifting moments in the course of a week. Those shifts can be smooth, or they can be as rough as my assaults on our car's clutch when my wife taught me how to drive a standard-shift Chevy in the 1970s. Teachers would do well to give some thought to the many transition points during the course of a day; they can be successful or there can be much grinding of gears, accompanied by the odd sotto voce muttering and a high degree of upsetness.

Here is what I have suggested to teachers on many occasions over the years. When a transition point is coming up, commit to taking the time to pause, get the attention of your students, *then* give the instruction(s) in a command voice, one that is quite different from your approachable (conversational) voice. Here are the steps the teacher in the example above could have taken to avoid the resultant unpleasantness everyone experienced between activities:

- **Step 1:** Does the board need to be erased at this moment? If so, do it quickly, then turn around and face the students with your hands at your sides.

- **Step 2:** Bring your palms up and face them in toward you, saying, "Look this way please." That reversing of your palms toward you is congruent with your command. Your combination of the visual with the auditory should bring them back to you.

- **Step 3:** Reach over and pick up a student journal. Hold it up and say, "Open your journals to where you left off yesterday." (Hand the journal you are holding back to the student.)

- **Step 4:** Explain what you want them to do.

Everything you do in steps 1 through 3 is pure process. Get the process elements down before moving on. Also, switch voices from your conversational/approachable voice (which you and your students were using while brainstorming) to your command/credible voice (a strong, but not necessarily loud, voice that drops off at the end). Conversational voices rise and fall in pitch and volume, but commands are short and unambiguous. There is no emotion, but lots of eye contact. Once the command is given, continue to make eye contact and wait until everyone

THE SMOOTH SHIFTING OF TRANSITIONAL GEARS

is looking at you. It is sometimes difficult to wait, but if students get the idea that looking at you is just a suggestion, the transition will become less efficient—and take longer—with time. Remember that silence, as we have seen, is also an attention getter.

The use of your command voice tells your students that an action on their part is required. This is a routine, by the way, that is important enough to practice several times during the first week of school. If done properly, there can be no question that everyone heard you. If you are facing the board or looking out the window when you tell them to look your way, the message is sent that whatever follows may not be important.

Build a Better Classroom Practicing Transitions

The most common transitions in an interactive classroom are those related to having students stand, move, pair, and share. Steps 1–5 below are process-oriented, while step 6 (the actual activity/conversation) is content-centered. Here are possible commands for the six steps:

- **Step 1:** Your goal here is to get them out of their seats and standing without anything in their hands. Face them with your hands at your sides, and say, "Everyone, please stand behind your desk and face me." (To make your gesture congruent with your command, bend over a bit, place your hands below your waist with your palms up, and stand up straight, raising your palms up to shoulder level in front of you. If they accomplish the transition quickly and efficiently, have them sit back down and do it again—and again until they get this down.)
- **Step 2:** "Thank you. When I say 'go,' spread out throughout the classroom in any open area. Go!" (Spread your arms to indicate the expanse of the room.) "Spread out a bit."
- **Step 3:** Wait until they are spread out. "Please face me." (Palms at face level and turned in toward you.)
- **Step 4:** Once they are all facing you, you can say, "Raise your right hand high, go two or three steps in any direction, and

shake hands with a classmate. This is your partner for this activity."

- **Step 5:** Once everyone has a partner, it is likely that they will be chatting a bit, and that is okay. Then, with palms about shoulder level and turned in toward you, say, "Please face me." (And wait until they are all facing you.)

- **Step 6:** This is where you can tell them what is going to happen.

  Again, the first five steps are process-oriented, designed to get everyone in standing pairs and facing you. When they stand behind their chairs, you will be checking to make sure they don't have anything in their hands. Once they are on their feet and spread out, returning things to their desks takes time away from the activity. My experience is that every time you go through these steps, the amount of time it takes to get to step 6 will shorten.

Give some thought before each week begins about the transition points that require a shifting of gears on your part:

- What is the most effective way to shift gears between the bell ringer and the first activity?

- Is there space in the classroom for fifteen standing pairs; if not, how can you rearrange the furniture to make that happen?

- What is the best way to get students from their seats into standing pairs?

- What is the simplest transition from that writing activity they just spent ten minutes on to the group work involving stations?

- What piece of upbeat music can be used to move them from poster to poster in the gallery walk?

- How many steps will it take to get them in standing quartets with their reflective journals and pencils in hand?

- What single, verbal and/or visual command will I use every time I want their attention? (In chapter 36, we'll explore ways to get the attention of students every time.)

CHAPTER 24
AVOID UNNECESSARY DECISIONS

We want students to learn to make good decisions in the classroom, on the playground, and in the cafeteria. We want them to make excellent choices when it comes to making progress toward learning targets. We and their parents want them to graduate with the ability to make good life decisions as well. And parents certainly want teachers to make good decisions when it comes to their own children. Kids learn to make decisions based on the available evidence, and they learn to unearth new information that can affect those decisions. Coaches want players who can, with their help, make excellent choices when game time comes around.

When it comes to nuts-and-bolts instructional processes, however, there are things teachers can—unintentionally—do that can derail the learning process, slow it down, or cause confusion on the part of students. An example would be the teacher who, again quite unintentionally, gives insufficient directions for the completion of a task, or gives too many verbal directions at once, overloading the short-term memory of sixth graders who may want to do the right thing but can't for the life of them remember what instructions they were given—they may be afraid to ask for clarification, so they muddle on regardless. It may take the teacher, as she walks around the room, several minutes to figure out things have gone awry, and too often, they can blame the students because they did not "pay attention" when the instructions were given.

When students make decisions based on a lack of information or insufficient clarity when it comes to what the expectations are, they often fail, then blame themselves. When it comes to a term paper, a simple checklist can do wonders in terms of the processes necessary for

CHAPTER 24

the successful completion of the task. Verbal directions, or even written directions given upfront, are insufficient. Process is important. Clarity is important. Confidence on the part of students is important, and it is affected by unforced errors on the part of teachers, errors that are preventable and unnecessary. Here is another example, and one that I suspect the reader—veteran student that you are—can identify with in looking back over many years in countless classrooms.

An eighth-grade language arts teacher displays a couple of paragraphs on the electronic white board. Some, perhaps not all, of the students begin reading the text as the teacher moves from her computer to one side of the screen. She begins to read the copy out loud to the class in a way that is her habit. But I am watching the students, not the teacher or the screen. The students who are in the process of reading the text on their own have now been interrupted by the teacher. Students will need to decide what to do, and do it quickly:

1) They can continue to read on their own, blocking out the teacher's voice because they are close to the end.

2) They can quit reading and try to listen to what the teacher is reading.

3) They can simply give up and disconnect altogether.

Herein lies the problem for students: The minute the image appears on the screen, they have one of two choices. They can ignore the text and wait for what they are pretty sure will happen—that is, the teacher will read it to them. Or, because almost anything visual draws their attention, they will give in to the temptation to read the copy to themselves. The decision has been forced on them by the teacher. The teacher knows what she wants to do, but the students may not be clear on this. The decision to do what comes naturally may cause confusion and even *resentment* on the part of those language arts students. We don't like being interrupted, frankly, and teachers need to take this into account.

Here is a scenario that would have taken the decision out of their hands: Next to a blank and darkened screen, the teacher faces the students, gets their attention, and gives the following instructions: "In a moment, you are going to see some text on someone who is an important figure in this story. I'll let you read this silently on your own. When you are done, just look up." And she takes one or two steps back as she reveals what she wants *them* to read. No confusion. No decision is necessary. There is no resentment, because the directions are clear. (By reading silently along with the students at a deliberate pace, by the way, the teacher can best judge when most of them will be done. I learned this from experience as well, with students and adults.) When the students are done reading, the teacher can darken the screen and move on. (Leaving an image on the screen, unless you are going to highlight a sentence or specific thought, will create unnecessary competition for your attention.)

Remember something about visuals, and we'll look at this in more detail in chapter 31: They always win.

- If the teacher starts talking while a visual image is still on the screen, it will serve as a distraction.

- If you are finishing an important point as you talk to your students, don't reveal the visual until you are done talking.

- When you reveal a visual, let them take it all in before you explain it. If you start talking as you display it, that choice comes into play again: Do they listen to you, or do they focus on the chart, graph, photo, or whatever copy has been revealed?

My advice is to avoid making them choose. Make *your* decisions as you do your planning, so students are not forced to make theirs later on.

Build a Better Classroom by Staying Clear of Forced Decisions

When you are running through your lesson on your own or with colleagues who are going to present the same lesson as part of your PLC experience, think not just about the big ideas, but about the nuts-and-bolts process elements. Spend some time with transition points, pondering what will happen if you give this set of verbal directions. How will you support verbal directions with visual instructions, and when will you reveal those? Think about that visual that is a critical component of the lesson.

CHAPTER 24

- How will you introduce it?
- When will you reveal it?
- When will you make it disappear?
- Do you need to bring the visual back, and if so, when?
- Do students need a paper copy? If so, when will they receive it? (If they receive it up front, they will do what comes naturally; they will look it over. It is best, if they need a handout of some sort, to give them a minute to look it over and familiarize themselves with it. They are going to do that anyway, and you can avoid trying to compete with that.)

CHAPTER 25
TRANSFER SKILLS TO THE COLLABORATIVE SETTING

As more teachers, schools, and districts move toward making project-based learning an integral part of the education of every student, there are skills that can be developed upfront in the school year that will help student groups function well in a PBL format. An example of this would be listening skills (eye contact, paraphrasing, and asking questions to clarify something, supportive body language, etc.). Whole-class discussions or group collaboration can come to a screeching halt if students have not practiced the skills related to active listening. I once heard a student in one group say, "Well, that's just stupid!" in response to what one of his peers had offered by way of an opinion. Such comments are not likely to move the group forward.

Once a project is completed, students may be asked to present to a group of adults, peers, or the school board. This requires a whole set of presentation skills that include speaking, listening, and the proper use of visuals such as charts and graphs, along with PowerPoint or some other presentation program. Students can practice powerful listening and speaking skills in pairs before moving into small groups. It is in pairs that students can learn to pause before asking or answering a question, treat a partner with respect, use the correctly pronounced names of classmates, interact with empathy, and learn from the perspectives of diverse partners.

Because projects are centered around a driving question, groups will likely, according to Bender (2012), use brainstorming "in order to generate ideas about how the PBL group may wish to initiate and complete that task" (p. 130). There are many brainstorming procedures, and teachers can choose which of these to introduce to the class. My experience is that it won't be enough to explain the procedure to students, put the steps on

CHAPTER 25

a poster, and turn the groups loose. Brainstorming is something teachers will need to have students practice in a whole-class setting.

Bender (2012) lists several brainstorming skills that are essential and that must be explained and worked through at the direction of the teacher. They include the following:

- Identify, consider, and stick to a broad topic without ranging too far afield.
- List all ideas without any initial editing or elimination of the concepts.
- Encourage others to think independently and differently about the topic.
- Respect all ideas as worthy of some consideration.
- Hold a closing phase in which ideas are compared and synthesized (i.e., placing two ideas together if they represent the same broader idea and if the person suggesting those ideas agrees to place them together as one idea).
- Demonstrate encouragement and respect for all discussion participants. (p. 131)

I have been in many groups of adults where the above skills proved invaluable. I have also seen the group process break down because the skills Bender mentions were not used. If student groups are expected to work independently on complex projects, they need to master skill sets related to cooperation, collaboration, active and empathetic listening, and decision-making.

Again, let me say, as I have said so many times in books and presentations, *begin with standing pairs*. My experience over decades of observing classrooms at all levels is that this is the basic unit of communication and collaboration. If students can learn to work with everyone in the room in pairs, they will learn names, get to know classmates, learn how to take care of partners (by listening and not judging), and build valuable skill sets related to face-to-face communication that will serve them well in groups—and in life.

Educators can be forgiven, perhaps, if they think that education today is all about the answers. Multiple choice questions are great examples of convergent thinking, where everything points in one direction. There is one answer; the student's job is to separate it from the incorrect choices. Project-based learning involves students in divergent thinking, where there are many possible directions students could go from the driving question at the center of the experience. This is why brainstorming is so important, and it is why the questions teachers ask when they approach a group are often more important than the answers.

Formative assessment is often all about observing and listening. Science teacher Rebecca Newburn maintains that formative assessment is about the questions. "When students are having discussions about their learning," write Boss and Larmer (2018), "she'll listen, ask probing questions, 'and then step back and let kids have the conversation. I'm not exactly a fly on the wall, but I'll only step in if I hear something that needs to be revisited or is a misconception'" (p. 115). If we want kids to figure things out, we have to let them figure things out.

Students also need to learn that feedback comes from many sources, and that includes peers and myriad available resources other than the teacher. I have observed in classrooms where the teacher wears herself out running from group to group, answering questions that could have been worked out at the local level. I have also observed classrooms where the teacher moved slowly from group to group, asking probing questions as a way of finding out where that particular group was in relation to the learning target. In these cases, hands don't shoot up like popping popcorn. I have moved from group to group in those classrooms as well. The difference between smooth-running groups and those that are largely dysfunctional often lies in the groundwork teachers do upfront when it comes to collaborative skill sets built around effective communication and a respect for diverse opinions and ideas.

Build a Better Classroom by Transferring Learned Skills to Collaborative Groups

Here are some ideas to ensure students have the collaboration and communication skills they need when they begin working on PBL tasks:

CHAPTER 25

- The Speaking and Listening Skills of the Common Core offer a great place to start when it comes to developing oral-language skills, and it begins in kindergarten. Some vertical planning might be in order here. Middle school teachers and administrators can let their counterparts at the 9–12 level know what they can expect students to be able to do when it comes to the kinds of skills students will need as they take that last step toward graduating into a world that highly values writing, thinking, and oral-language skills.

- When students involved in PBL tasks and projects are expected to present to adult audiences, teachers and administrators can pull together an adult audience from within the building, the district, or the community so that student teams can practice their presentations in a setting similar to the one they'll encounter when it is time to present more formally. Several years ago, I was part of a group offering feedback to a group of eighth graders doing just that.

- A great many schools now mandate class meetings to begin the day, and in Malibu Elementary School in Virginia Beach, teachers use those twenty-minute sessions to teach valuable social skills that will come in handy for the rest of the day as students communicate and collaborate in pairs and groups.

CHAPTER 26
PROVIDE EASY ACCESS TO COMPLEX TASKS

When I first started teaching, sometime in the Dark Ages, all my students needed was the textbook, a number 2 pencil, and a notebook. That's it, for the simple reason that my students had two basic tasks on most days: Listen and take notes. I did the talking. I did the explaining. I did the research. Mine was *not* an interactive classroom; it was an *inactive* classroom. The bar was low in terms of the kinds of access students needed to materials, staff, or technology.

I was the one to whom they went with questions. I provided the feedback. I provided the answers. They did not need access to working computers; there were none. They did not need a corner of the room where they could practice a presentation in front of peers; they and all their peers were in student desks facing me. They did not need access to each other at tables or in quads with student desks pulled together; I spent a good deal of time saying, "Do your own work." Learning and practicing oral language skills was for speech class, and that was an elective at the high school level.

In the highly interactive classrooms of today, students have more responsibility and more autonomy. One group of four students may be working on a presentation that will be given to the school board next Thursday. Another group is doing some research that requires the use of a couple of computers. While the teacher is talking with one group, other students may be seeking feedback and other assistance from fellow students.

Interactive classrooms are busy and often noisy places, and teachers need to make sure that students have access to everything they will need to succeed. I was in a classroom where students spent a good deal

CHAPTER 26

of time trying to boot up a computer; the computer could have been up and ready to go. Students can—and should—know which classmates are the go-to experts on grammatical principles. The teacher who gives a set of instructions composed of six steps can—and should—make that set of instructions visible for the entire class period, and available online after hours. Students working on persuasive essays can—and should—know where to go to read several anchor essays. Collaborative groups can—and should—have easy access to the norms that were set up at the beginning of the year, norms that underpin the smooth functioning of groups.

Teachers who want to be able to circulate from group to group or student desk to student desk don't want to have to turn on a computer, rummage around in a file drawer for an anchor essay, remind students of the directions for the task, answer questions that could have been answered had the student known which of his peers was an expert on the information, or any number of things related to student access. I have seen teachers spend much too much time troubleshooting and running needless errands for students. When I started teaching, I was the source; I was the go-to person for almost everything.

Interactive classrooms require easy access for students who have a limited amount of time to get something done but should not have limited access to what they need. This means teachers need to plan ahead in ways I and my colleagues would have found unnecessary. If we want students to be responsible as they problem solve, complete sometimes complicated tasks and projects, and prepare in groups for an important presentation, the road to continuous improvement should be paved with easy access to necessary materials, information, tools, directions, and answers to any number of questions.

I have seen classrooms where it is apparent that a great deal of preparation went into getting everything ready for six groups of four in each of four classes to work collaboratively on various projects. I have also seen classrooms where teachers spend the class period in search of this or that piece of information, document, markers, or the anchor essay that "I know is around here somewhere." Teachers would do well to spend some time thinking through what students are likely to need, based on what individuals or groups are working on at the moment.

PROVIDE EASY ACCESS TO COMPLEX TASKS

Build a Better Classroom with Access

Here are some things you can do to help things run smoothly and let you concentrate on observing, listening, asking guiding questions, coaching, and providing feedback when necessary:

- Where iPads are plentiful, but teachers who want to maintain a highly interactive environment can see to it that the IT specialist provides enough platforms for half the students in the room; the teacher can then put students in pairs on one platform. Students working in pairs on projects need only one platform to get the job done, and they are getting experience at working together to accomplish the task.
- I have observed classrooms in which scissors, markers, glue sticks, etc. are available in jars or cans in one location. One middle school teacher provided a heavy plastic zip bag that she fastened to the side of each student desk, holding those basic materials, thus making students responsible for their own supplies, while reducing the amount of time necessary to prepare for an activity.
- Keep directions you have already given verbally on the screen while students work. Rather than raising their hands to ask you questions related to the process, students can simply glance at the visual image.
- If they are writing sentences, paragraphs, essays, or term papers, have anchors easily accessible, and not hidden away in a file drawer. And a checklist doesn't have to be distributed on paper; it can be displayed on the smartboard. Out of twenty-six students in the classroom, someone will have misplaced his printed reference sheet.
- One fifth-grade teacher kept a large container filled with sharpened pencils on her desk. The pencils were there because one student's job at the end of each day was to pick them up, sharpen them, and return them to the container. Other students

CHAPTER 26

were tasked with straightening the furniture, erasing the board, and other tasks that had the room ready for the next day.

- Designate (with their permission) students as the go-to "experts" on certain things. One teacher told me her "aha moment" came when she realized she wasn't the only teacher in the room.

- On days when students will be highly interactive and moving around the room frequently, arrange the furniture in such a way that they have easy access to various stations they will all be using at one time or another, or access to wall charts in a carousel activity.

- Train students in the art of coaching. If a student from one group gets up to go and help another group, giving them the answer is less powerful than asking questions or revealing clues or information that will help the group arrive at their own conclusions or the correct answer.

CHAPTER 27
THE FIRST FEW MINUTES

For students, the first few minutes of class sends one of two messages: (1) This is going to be a great experience, or (2) This is going to be the same-old-same-old. It is the teacher who sends and controls the message. The teacher can enter the room as if he is carrying a great weight, or he can close the door with a smile on his face, having greeted everyone by name as they entered. I have seen teachers stand at the lectern taking roll by calling names out and placing a mark in the gradebook, following that impactful opening with, "Okay, open your textbooks to page 984." Students, veterans all, are pretty certain that page 984 does not contain much that is different from yesterday's page 976. In classrooms like this, the first few minutes look a lot like the middle few minutes and the last few minutes. The gradual transition from the beginning of class to the end is accompanied invariably by the glazing over of many pairs of eyes.

Ron Hoff (1992) gives presenters (and by extension, teachers-as-presenters) some timeless advice: "Never hesitate to let your audience know that you're delighted that they're there." This applies to classrooms, too, and with the same possible caveat, according to Goff: "You'd better mean it!" (p. 30). Students are nothing if not perceptive, and they know an imposter when they see one. They'll spot an insincere smile or hollow laughter a mile off, or at least from the back row.

I watched one morning as a middle school teacher entered the classroom, moved to the power position (front and center), opened her arms, and said, "Have I got a story for you!" She said that in a way that made me, a stranger on loan from central office, *want to hear that story*. It was a personal story that had nothing whatever to do with the subject matter, but it drew veritable bouts of laughter from everyone in the room. She

CHAPTER 27

high-fived someone in the front row, then moved on into the day's activities. Laughter, says Tate (2012), "can be considered a form of internal jogging" because it increases blood flow and lowers stress-hormone levels (p. 48). "Have I got a story for you!" easily beats, "Turn to page 984." as an opener in any classroom.

One great motivator for students entering the classroom is a teacher who greets them at the door in the kind of good mood they have come to expect, not eliciting a comment along the lines of "Is that a smile I see on his face???" Being in a good mood for our students—or not—is a choice. I have always recommended teachers begin their day with the music they love, on the way to school and inside the classroom, while getting ready for the arrival of students. "The ability for songs to deliver an emotional lift is one of the main reasons that music is one of the constants of the modern human experience—why we spend our lives literally surrounded by music" (Allen and Wood, 2013, p. 24). Songs are mood lifters for everyone, including students, and one way to get toes tapping and neurotransmitters flowing for them is to play some upbeat music as they come into the classroom.

Many teachers will stand in the hallway and chat with colleagues from down the hall, and on occasion, students can hear them complaining about something better left unsaid, at least in a busy hallway full of kids. The mood created by that unfortunate and unnecessary conversation may well carry over into the first few minutes of class. Those precious minutes between periods at the secondary level can be put to better use making students feel welcome and appreciated, and this helps build those positive relationships that are so important in a learning community.

Build a Better Classroom at the Opening Bell

On entering the room, the best teachers I have observed over the years didn't find it necessary to talk over the students to get their attention at the beginning of the class period. They didn't gesticulate wildly; they simply walked to the power position up front and stood still. Bob Garmston, in *The Astonishing Power of Storytelling* (2019), encourages presenters to "be centered" and "appear grounded and calm" before a public appearance. Teaching certainly qualifies as a (daily) public appearance, I would argue.

THE FIRST FEW MINUTES

Garmston would agree that in your role as learner-in-chief as you enter your classroom, you can take a couple of deep breaths, drop your arms to your sides, spreading your feet apart in a comfortable stance, "imagine that you are pushing both feet into the floor, then release that tension" (pp. 83–84). The whole idea is to get physically and mentally ready for your roles as presenter, storyteller, facilitator, and coach. Those first few minutes are critically important in terms of building and nurturing relationships with students.

Here are some reflective questions that can be shared with a teacher friend, or in a small group of colleagues:

- Why is it important to start class on time?
- Why are the first few minutes of class so important?
- What songs could be played as students enter the classroom as mood lifters?
- Can the nature and structure of bell ringers be changed from time to time so that students do not see the "same-old-same-old" opening routine every day? Could the bell ringer, traditionally done sitting down, be followed immediately by a standing pair share or a gallery walk to get students up, moving, and sharing?

CHAPTER 28
LAST IMPRESSIONS

Students enter and leave your classroom every day, and those transition points should be as memorable as you can make them. My students' last impressions of my classes include flinging memorable closing lines at them as they headed for the exit: "Wait!! Don't forget to read section 5 tonight!" or "Hunker down tonight for that test tomorrow!!!" On occasion, I would lecture right up until the bell rang, saying, "My, time just seems to fly in here, doesn't it?" It is possible they did not share my sentiments. It is possible my class closes did not leave them wanting more. They may have wanted more fire drills.

The last few minutes of a class period, a block, or a full day in elementary school should be put to good use, and they should be planned carefully and executed faithfully. What you do at the end leaves an impression as they prepare to go where everyone has gone before, to the next class, to the gym, to lunch, to the restroom, or to volleyball practice. As with a speech or a concert, what we remember most may be what is done last. Hopefully, what is done last may leave them believing that this class and this teacher are somehow refreshingly different.

Laughter and music release neurotransmitters that serve as mood enhancers, and both can be used to close out the class period, block, or day. One school whose mascot is the bulldog plays "Who let the dogs out?" at the end of the day. Two fifth-grade teachers used to use Roy Orbison's *Pretty Woman* to line their students up as they got ready to leave for the next class. Frankly, leaving a classroom while listening to a great piece of music beats, "Don't forget that you all owe me a term paper on Friday!!!!" every time.

CHAPTER 28

I know teachers who use that last five minutes on a Friday to get feedback from students as to how things went for them this week. If each student has two blank sticky notes, he or she can record what went well for them on one sticky, and record something that was confusing or otherwise unclear on the other. Feedback from over a hundred middle school students can allow a teacher to make adjustments in the weeks ahead. My experience is that students appreciate teachers who ask for their feedback, and then follow up, letting them know that this or that change is due to their valuable input. If students don't believe a teacher has read the first batch of sticky notes, they are less likely to provide input on a second occasion. If, however, they come to believe the teacher is really listening and acting on the feedback, then they are more likely to participate when they are asked to do so.

That last five minutes can be devoted to stories—yours and theirs. If you are trying to impress upon them the importance of making mistakes in the continuous improvement process, why not share a couple of your own mistakes—professional or personal—that helped you make a needed adjustment. Why not have a coach come in and share why mistakes are so important from a team standpoint? How about having students share their stories as well? How about sharing stories of empathy? How about a story about the importance of perspectives?

My point here, I guess, is that the class period, the block, or the school day should not end with a finger-wagging admonition to study harder, hunker down, get those assignments in, or improve behavior. I did all those things in my classrooms, and I rarely gave any thought to how to close in a way that made my kids look forward to the next day. Musicians save the best for last. Too often, teachers save the best for the weekend.

Build a Better Classroom with a Memorable Close

Last impressions can be powerful or nonexistent. Students can leave the room laughing, or they can leave the laughter until after school. The act of standing sends more blood to the brain, carrying with it oxygen and glucose—the latter for energy; standing to discuss something for a couple of minutes at the end of the period or the end of the day can be invigorating. The sharing of ideas and the sharing of stories can be a pick-me-up to send students out the door or out to the bus. My suggestion is that teachers give some thought to those last few minutes. A great opening and a great ending to the class period can serve as positive bookends to an eventful class period or day.

It is possible, even probable, that there are some great ways to leave lasting impressions used by other teachers in the building. These questions could be posted on a building-based or district-wide blog, or they could be the sole topic of a faculty meeting:

- How do you close out your classes each day?

- How can your lessons be adjusted so that there is a five-minute change-of-pace activity or message at the end?

- How can you use that time, at least on some days, to solicit useful feedback from students?

- How can you use music, stories, or humor to send students off to their next stop in the building?

- How can that last five minutes be used to develop communication skills and life skills for students who will need both?

CHAPTER 29
THAT'S THE PLAN

Students today often find themselves creating presentations with their peers as the culmination of a project-based learning endeavor. Those can include charts, graphs, and presentation programs using PowerPoint or some other piece of presentation software. This chapter offers a few suggestions for teachers-as-presenters and for students faced with making a presentation to peers or adults, or both. I'll concentrate on the presentation program here, and not with speaking or listening skills as such.

Students may be asked to present in front of adults or students from other classes. I watched a class full of eighth graders practice for a presentation to the school board. Their project was to create a plan for a new soccer pitch, complete with the right grass, a concession stand, stands for spectators, lighting, and everything a contractor might need to deal with for that project. Competitions for groups like DECA require a great deal of preparation on the part of student teams. Most presentations would likely be in front of student audiences composed of classmates, and visuals are important. Student presenters need to pay close attention to visuals, whether they be charts or electronic presentation software programs.

When creating the slides as part of the presentation program, keep the verbiage short and the graphics simple. The more you include on a slide, the less they will remember. Avoid using too many colors; the colors become the message and the message is lost. I have seen charts and slides with excellent graphs and charts that were in black only, with no color that might serve as a distraction. The message should never be shouldered aside by slides that are too complex to understand, with copy that is too long to read, or with a set of complex graphics that require a great deal of time to decipher.

Remind students preparing to present to an audience that the amount of time it takes to run through the slides in their presentation should be far less than the amount of time they have been given by the people who have invited them to present. If, for example, time is to be left for questions, plan for it. Here are some things students will need to anticipate as they put together their slide presentation:

- They will want to give audience members time to answer questions at some point, probably at the end. If the end is where they want the questions, the student who kicks off the presentation can ask that questions be held until they are finished.

- As we will see in chapter 31, visuals always win; if the slide on the screen is not needed while a presenter is talking, go to black with it, using the remote. Don't let the visual compete with the auditory. Visuals that distract from an important verbal message create dissonance.

- If the presenter is part of a group, visit the venue of your final presentation if you can, or get someone to send pictures of the presentation venue. Part of the planning process is to become familiar with the room, along with the following:
    1. Is there built-in seating, as in a district school board room, and a specific place for the presenters to stand and move about?
    2. Is there a built-in screen; if so, how large is it? (If the audience is going to be composed of a dozen or so people, a few chairs upfront in a semi-circle will suffice, and the students will NOT want eighty chairs for twelve people, if possible. If the eighty chairs must be there, then pull the front row up a bit, put it in a semi-circle, and place a handout on each of the twelve chairs. Have someone greet the members of the audience as they come in, indicating they should be seated on any chair with a handout.)

PLANNING THE PRESENTATION

3. If there are monitors connected to your laptop or to the site's computer, make sure you run through the program to make certain that what you display on the screen can be seen from the back row.

4. What is the sound system like? (Students who have never used a microphone will want to practice and get used to how far away it should be held from the mouth, and where the volume should be set on the amplifier unit.)

5. Is there a built-in projector/computer in the room? (If so, students should put their presentation on TWO flash drives, with one as a backup, and run through all of the slides in the presentation. On occasion, I have found that graphic images can be distorted in going from a laptop to another unit, especially if one is going from an Apple unit to a PC. If there is no built-in system, what arrangements will you/they need to make?)

6. Where will those who are not presenting at any given time stand, sit, or kneel? (They must be close enough to move quickly and confidently to where they need to stand, replacing a teammate without bumping into him or her. They should not be so close that they will serve as a distraction while another member of the team presents.)

7. What is the lighting system like, and how is it controlled? (Your students do not want to find out three minutes before they present that the fluorescent or IED bulbs right in front of the screen are going to wash out the image. To be forewarned is to be forearmed.)

8. Finally, try to put together an audience composed of students and/or adults to preview the presentation and provide feedback. (If you can present in the venue where the actual presentation will take place, so much the better.) During the practice session, invite members of the audience to write down comments or questions that can serve as valuable feedback when the presentation is finished. If

you have time, chart the feedback. If not, collect the written feedback from audience members before they leave. My suggestion is that you let them deal with the feedback themselves and you can ask them later how the debrief went.

Team members should become completely familiar with the presentation itself, along with any equipment they may be using. If a chart stand and white chart paper are needed, get students familiar with them early. Charts and chart stands are old-school, but they can be very effective *for that very reason*. The brain responds well to novelty, and charts and chart stands qualify as such in the twenty-first century.

As we discovered in chapter 6, redundancy is our friend when it comes to presentations for teachers and students alike. A box with extra markers, batteries, another remote for the laptop or computer, and a second microphone in case the first one is found to be defective, even with a new battery. (Always insert fresh batteries in anything you are using that requires them.)

One final note on handouts. I do not simply print out my PowerPoint with three or six slides to the page and give everyone a copy. If the audience is in possession of the entire presentation upfront, why attend? This is why conference goers often move from session room to session room, collecting handouts. If a handout can be made interactive in nature, so that participants can make lists, jot down questions for later, or take a few notes themselves, that is fine. The presentation can always be provided in printed form as they leave or when the team is done presenting.

Build a Better Presentation with Proper Planning and Practice

One final thought on student presentations as part of a PBL unit: Whenever attendees can be turned into participants, you might suggest your students do this. Attendees attend, but participants learn, and students-as-presenters can ask participants to turn to a partner and process something or answer a question. Participants can be asked to pair up to discuss something related to the subject of the presentation as a way of providing context. One of the presenters can even invite participants to stand at the end and, in pairs, come up with a couple of questions.

As students put together their presentation, help them understand that just talking for twenty-five minutes will elicit the same reaction teachers get when they talk for twenty-five minutes while students sit; audience members may go elsewhere in their minds. Great presentations turn attendees into participants as much as possible. Great presenters practice as much as possible. Great teachers model excellent presentation skills all the time.

CHAPTER 30
IF THE FONT FITS, SHARE IT

Every educator who uses a presentation program in a classroom or conference session has decisions to make concerning fonts, type sizes, the amount of text displayed at any one time, the complexity of graphics to accompany the text, and much else. Running down a list of fonts available can take a great deal of time, and many of them look like they might be interesting to an audience. There is one salient fact to remember about your presentation, whether you are presenting to a classroom full of kids or to an adult audience: Your number one presentation tool is your voice. What is on the screen is meant to support your message, not supplant it.

I have created hundreds of presentations over the past twenty-five years, and my rule of thumb when it comes to everything that will appear on the screen is this: Keep it simple. Tahoma, a sans-serif font, is clean and uncomplicated, as are Arial and Calibri. When preparing a presentation using PowerPoint, I put myself in the shoes—or chairs—of participants. I don't want them staring at an unusual and highly decorative type font for the entire presentation. The font should not be the *focus* for students in the classroom or for the adults in a faculty meeting. The words help convey the overarching message. Again, keep it simple.

If a paragraph or several sentences are key to your lesson, make sure they, too, are projected with a font size that is eminently readable from all over the classroom. I have participated in workshops where participants struggled to read what was on the screen, to the point where they would ask someone next to them, "What does that say?" Unfortunately, if it can't be read, it doesn't say anything, other than that the proper preparation for the lesson or presentation was simply lacking.

CHAPTER 30

If there is something on the screen you want your students to read, stay still and let them read it. If you are walking around the room or rummaging in your desk, this causes a distraction. And don't read it to them. If they are trying to read what you have projected on the screen while you read it, this creates dissonance, and the message gets lost in the resulting confusion.

In highly interactive classrooms and conference sessions, participants will be up, moving, pairing, and sharing in all parts of the room. As participants sit or stand facing the screen, they should be able to read every slide without having to squint or ask someone near them what it says. Yet I have seen professional presenters display a slide with several sentences, paragraphs, or bulleted items in 12- or 14-point type, then say the following: "I realize you can't read this, but . . ." Here is a bit of unsolicited advice: If you know they won't be able to read it, *don't put it in the presentation*. Use a few bullet points of 28-point type or larger, and speak to those points. There is no need to apologize, something that is embarrassing to the participants, if we prepare the presentation with the audience—students or adults—in mind.

Here is something I did when I first got started in the business of presenting full time. Using the sans-serif font Tahoma, I typed the same sentence several times using various type sizes from 18 points on up to maybe 36 points; each sentence was centered and they were stacked from the top of the slide to the bottom. Projecting it on a large screen in a school cafeteria, I walked around the room in an area about the size of what I would be using when I presented to a teacher audience down the road a bit. This proved to me in black and white that my range would be from 28- to 44-point type for all my presentations. What I saw is what they would see, and that settled it for me. The bottom line here is this: Time spent on putting yourself in the shoes—and seats—of your students is time well spent.

Build a Better Classroom with Effective Visual Support

The next time you are a participant in a conference or professional-development session, pay close attention to the presentation program, taking a few notes and answering these questions:

IF THE FONT FITS, SHARE IT

- Is the type font simple (and not a distraction by itself)?
- Are all the font sizes displayed on the screen readable, or are some too small?
- If the presenter suddenly realizes that the font size that looked readable on his computer is too small for anyone in the audience to read, do they apologize *but stay with the slide*?
- Does the presenter, at times (or a great deal of the time), simply read verbatim what is on the screen?
- Are there [annoying] typos on the screen?
- Is there too much on the screen to take in [before the next slide appears]?
- Does the lighting in the room wash out the image and the words?
- Does the type font itself overpower the message by being too hard to read (as it can be when presenters use a script font)?

Check off the things from the above list that drove you to distraction during a conference session or college night class. *Don't do those things*!

CHAPTER 31
VISUALS ALWAYS WIN
(MAKE THAT WORK FOR YOU!)

A teacher finishes a short lecture from the front of the room, then moves to her desk, giving her students a set of auditory directions while walking away from them. On the face of it, there is nothing wrong here; her directions may have been clearly stated. Unfortunately, they were lost on a fairly large number of her students. Had she asked someone at random to repeat the directions she had given just a few moments ago, chances are many of her students would have been unable to do so.

Again, the problem here is not with the directions themselves. The difficulty is that when the teacher began to move from where she was to a point behind her desk, the students' concentration was broken by the movement itself. As John Medina (2008) asserts, the visual always trumps the auditory. The teacher could have avoided the confusion on the part of students by simply moving to the power position (front and center), making eye contact with students while saying, "Pause, look this way please." She could also have used the movement of her hands—hands up and palms forward when she said, "Pause . . ." followed by the palms turned inward, toward herself, when she said, "look this way please." Her command voice and her hand movements would have gotten their attention. Her final step would have been to wait until everyone had finished talking and was facing her.

At that point, and with their complete attention, she could have given a short set of auditory directions. Then the problem becomes that they can't hold five directions in their minds all at once and keep them there

CHAPTER 31

until they have carried them out. The next step on her part would have been to reveal the directions on the screen in order and *leave them there* until they were no longer needed. The visual would have supplemented the auditory.

I have also seen, and I have used this on occasion myself, teachers who will forego the auditory directions, face the screen from the side, and hit the remote on the laptop or a button on the screen to reveal the directions, with no auditory support whatsoever. I saw this used in a high school classroom, and it was obvious that the teacher used this method of giving directions frequently. What she wanted them to do next was then added in large black type on the screen, *and she did not compete with the visual by saying a word.* She let them (1) read the directions and (2) make them happen.

This brings me to another point concerning visual vs. auditory. Teachers like to talk, and those who talk too much discount what they are saying, for the simple reason that students tune them out, even though they may look at the teacher and smile. Watching body language can tell a classroom observer much, and it has told me on many occasions that the more teachers talk, the less students listen. The teacher who used visuals to provide directions went a long way toward adding impact to her words when she did talk.

Here are some ways in which teachers can cut down on teacher talk, including the most important of all—decrease it in favor of more student-to-student conversations!

- Pause for visuals: When displaying some text on the screen, don't read it. Let them read it. Let them look at and process any graphic image, including charts.

- Rather than explaining what they should see when looking at a picture or other image, put them in pairs and *let them discuss what they see.*

- When you use your cue to get them to stop talking and face you, don't say a word until the last voice goes silent and they are facing you. If you start talking while they continue to do so, you have just given them permission to do that every time.

- Give a single direction in large type on the screen: "Open your reflective journals to where you were writing yesterday." (Again, if you have been talking for some time, this visual represents a state change for them, and it commands their attention. There is no need to say anything until everyone has his or her journal open.)

- If you want them to clean off their desks, display a picture of a clean desk on the screen. If you want them to have only their notebooks on their desks, display a picture of a desk with a journal on it. This can be used for any desk—or lab—setup. (Remember, let the visual and the kids do the work. The less you use your voice, the more impact it has.)

In another example of the power of visuals, one I have witnessed on many occasions, a teacher or presenter moves in front of the screen facing the students in a classroom or the audience in a training session. They do not realize that they are between the projector and the screen. The image appears on the upper torso and forehead of the presenter, and as he or she moves slightly, different parts of the image materialize in a way that is decidedly disconcerting to the students or session participants. A white shirt is filled with text and whatever message the presenter is trying to convey is lost.

In yet another example of the visual riding roughshod over the auditory, teachers or session presenters will often reveal an image on the screen, then leave it there as they begin to talk. Whenever an image of any kind appears in front of a group of students or seminar participants, they will naturally want to check it out, look it over, and ponder its meaning. Most of what the teacher/presenter says at that point is lost. The words simply can't compete with a new and compelling graphic, picture, or piece of text. Visual wins every time.

CHAPTER 31

Build a Better Classroom with the Powerful Use of Visuals

PAUSE FOR VISUALS

Here are some actions teachers can take to increase the impact of the auditory in classrooms:

- If you display a set of directions on the screen, leave them in place as students begin work on a task or project. This leaves you free to work the room without six hands going up—all with the same question: "What am I supposed to do again?"

- When you are using a projection system and PowerPoint, or another program, use your remote to go black with the image while you move to the power position in the front of the room to talk about something. If the image is critical to an explanation you need to make, move to the side so you are not between the projector and the screen.

- When you reveal an image of any kind on the screen, give students time to check it out and digest its meaning. *Remember, if you try to compete with a visual, the visual will likely win.*

CHAPTER 32
ATTENTION TO VOICE

I never gave much thought to my voice when I embarked on my teaching career. It had, after all, served me pretty well in high school and in college. The difference, of course, and one that did not register with me at the time, is that beginning with my student-teaching experience, I shifted from being an attendee in most of my high school and college classes into presenter mode. Teachers spend a great deal of time in presenter mode, and the presenter's chief tool is his or her voice. Teachers-as-presenters ought to spend some time thinking about big little things such as volume, pitch, articulation, the use of the pause, and the rate of delivery.

Taking this last presentation attribute first, one of the things anyone listening to a presenter is likely to notice is how quickly or slowly the words are delivered. "If you speak too quickly," assert Bob Garmston and Bruce Wellman (1992), "your words run together and are difficult to decipher. If you speak too slowly, you lose your audience members as they fill in the gaps and pauses with their own thoughts or spend all their energy trying to guess your next words" (p. 64). One of the ways a teacher can determine how quickly or slowly he speaks is to tape himself and, in the viewing, revert to the role of participant. Hoff (1992), referring not to teachers but to presenters, says of the taping, "Spend a day or two with your own voice, and see if you're someone you would like to listen to" (p. 122). The word taping dates me, I know. Easier to simply find someone with a cell phone.

There are many attributes of an effective presenter on which one can focus when viewing thirty minutes or so of footage taken in the classroom. Because we are talking about voice here, I suggest turning off the picture

CHAPTER 32

while listening to the sound. Visuals, as we have seen, trump the auditory, and when I taped two of my classes decades ago, I kept getting caught up in my (frequent and distracting) physical gestures. Someone suggested I get rid of the picture and just listen to my voice, and that worked. I could concentrate on what I was saying, how quickly the words came out, and much else related to the auditory component of my delivery.

Many, perhaps most, teachers raise the volume of their voices when they want to make a point or emphasize something important. The frequency with which an increased volume is used makes it less effective than lowering one's voice for emphasis. I have seen presenters drop from a high decibel count to a whisper, something that is called the step-down. It is highly effective in connecting with the audience. Timing comes into play here, too. If you want to drop your voice precipitously in order to give emphasis to something, try pausing for a second before letting your voice fall into whisper mode for a few words or a sentence. Pausing builds tension (a good kind of tension) by making participants hang on that last word, wondering what will come next. Going from full volume to a whisper really does get the attention of participants, and it serves to underline the point.

With project-based learning becoming an ever more important part of the curriculum in districts, schools, and classrooms, it is important that students become better presenters. I have seen excellent student presentations, and some that would have been much better had they been trained and coached in the art of making presentations. If voice is the most important tool in the presenter's tool box, then teachers should not only model the powerful use of voice, but share that tool—and the whole tool box—with students.

As we saw in chapter 12, silence is a great tool for the presenter. Bob Garmston, the author of *The Presenter's Fieldbook* (2018), is a master presenter and group facilitator. When Garmston takes a question from the audience, he rarely provides an answer right away. He will pause, turn his head to the side, then face the person who asked the question before proceeding. His voice picks up the action again only after that *purposeful* moment of reflection for everyone in the room.

I've been fortunate enough to observe in hundreds of classrooms, and there is a phenomenon related to voice that finds its way into the opening minutes of class. Teachers using their own, natural voice with colleagues in the hallway will stand in front of the classroom and change it completely, raising the volume and pitch. Garmston and Wellman (1992) point out that "a relaxed and natural voice is a presenter's best friend" (p. 64). Students who have been with a teacher for several weeks or months know them well, and there is no need for teachers to use anything other than a genuine smile and a natural voice. Garmston and Wellman recommend that presenters relax their shoulders and the muscles in their necks. I have found that teachers who have an informal conversation or three with students at the door in a natural voice tend to keep that voice in place when they face the entire class. "Relax and be yourself" may not be bad advice after all.

Building a Better Classroom with Attention to Voice

Again, most teachers pay little attention to their voice. Because it is such a powerful tool, it can be made to work for you. It may also work against you if your voice tends to drop off at the end of a sentence or if you use the approachable voice when giving verbal directions in class. Students who are going to give presentations or speaking in whole-class discussions will also find that voice is a powerful tool for getting the message across.

- If you want to improve your use of voice, I suggest you find a colleague willing to spend maybe twenty to twenty-five minutes in your classroom observing that—and only that. The same can be done, of course, with other presentation skills (use of gestures, movement, etc.). Feedback is the lifeblood of continuous improvement.

- One way to make sure your voice is ready for your classroom in the morning is to spend some time talking with friends and colleagues before the students arrive.

- In terms of articulation and rate, consider getting feedback from students. Are you clearly understood by them? Are you speaking too quickly? Too slowly?

- Watch master presenters speak on TED Talk or on YouTube. Listen to how they use the pause, a drop in volume, and body language as they present.

CHAPTER 33
ARMS CONTROL

While teaching seventh-grade history in the early 1990s, I asked our librarian to videotape one of my classes. I did so with some trepidation, as I recall, but I wanted to see and hear what my students saw and heard every day. After loading the tape in the machine, I listened with the picture off, then watched with the sound off. In this latter mode, I was amazed, and not a little embarrassed, to see how much gesturing I did with my arms. I was reminded of a Pittsburgh policeman I once saw directing traffic at a busy intersection. As a result of that experience, I made an effort (not always successfully) to cut back on the use of gestures that distracted from the message I wanted to deliver.

There is something else I did, and I have seen this in classrooms all over the country over these many years. When a student raised his hand, I pointed directly at him and said, "Yes, Phil." I have since replaced the pointing finger of fate with an open palm. The open palm gesture is inclusive, not accusatory. Extending two open palms is a welcoming gesture, and the palms can face—and move—down toward the floor when inviting students to sit down after a stand-pair-share activity. The palms can face inward when instructing students to "Look this way, please." When I ask workshop participants to pause after they have been talking in pairs for a while, I say, "Pause" with my palms facing them, then I turn my palms in toward myself as I instruct them to look at me.

Simple hand and arm gestures, when used sparingly and consistently, can eventually be used without the auditory component. One of the best presenters I know will place his arms out, palms down, crouch a bit, then flip his palms and bring them up as he rises to his full height. He says

CHAPTER 33

nothing, but this is a clear signal to seated participants to stand in place. (This same gesture is used by an orchestra conductor when she wants the orchestra musicians to stand to be recognized.) When I want my workshop participants to be seated after standing for a while, I don't say anything; I just put my arms straight out, palms down, and lean over. This is my visual signal to sit down.

Controlled hand and arm gestures, used repeatedly for a specific purpose, can serve as an efficient and effective visual tool. Too much gesticulating can serve as a visual distractor, however, as students follow the movement while ignoring whatever the teacher is saying. There are many good reasons to record a lesson; using it to look for unnecessary and distracting arm gestures can help teachers with their presentation skills. The same is true of students working on their own PBL presentations. Students may, in fact, be much less anxious about recording presentations for posterity than teachers.

One seemingly small, but annoying, habit teachers let students get into has to do with the raising of hands to answer a question, ask one of their own, or provide some input during class. A teacher who asks for input may see three or four hands go up . . . and *stay* up even as the teacher calls on one student. All those raised but unemployed hands can cause a distraction. One of the best, most effective presenters I have ever seen, Bob Garmston, models a solution to what I have heard called "popcorn hands." Garmston will see four hands go up, and he will, palm out, put them in order by name: "Tony first, then Wilma, Scott, and Marie. Tony?" The key for the teacher is to remember the names and the order. Wilma will know she is second; heaven help Mrs. Desmond if she goes to Scott second, moving him in front of Wilma. The purpose of this, of course, is to keep all those distracting hands down.

Building a Better Classroom with Purposeful, Positive Gestures

Body language can be powerful; it can be positive or negative in tone. Crossing one's arms while listening to someone else may send the signal, "I'm not interested in what you are saying." The listener would certainly deny that, of course, but it is what the speaker interpreted that is important. Standing with hands on hips may indicate impatience to the speaker, even though the listener may not have meant it that way. When working with students on paired conversations, teachers can work with them on supportive body language (standing straight with palms at the sides, facing in), but my experience is that it takes practice. When I demonstrate this stance in workshops with adults, it sometimes takes all day, if I pursue it, to break bad habits.

Here are a few suggestions to help you maximize the positive impact of body language on your students:

- If you record one of your classes, I suggest you let your students know why you are doing it. Otherwise, they may think you want to put the spotlight on them.

- Rather than record a lesson, you could invite a colleague to sit in on one of your classes and look for gestures and body language in general. For example, I found that I crossed my arms when talking with a student. This is generally regarded as a body-language no-no; the student may interpret those entwined arms as a sign that you are not open to what she is saying.

- If your students are going to be giving presentations as the natural culmination of a project, part of their training in oral language skills can include gestures and body language.

- There are many speakers who appear on YouTube, and focusing not on their words, but on their gestures, can be informative and instructive. Some are disciplined in this regard, and others not so much.

- If you can find a video clip of a speaker in action, turn off the sound and, with your students, take some notes about gestures. Then watch the clip again with the sound on to see the gestures again and juxtapose them with the speaker's voice and message. Were there any gestures that were distracting? Were there some that seemed to support the speaker's message or help make a point?

CHAPTER 33

- Your gestures can serve as silent cues. Two fingers at your lips may indicate your students should stop talking. Two palms down may mean your students should sit on the rug. (These need to be modeled and practiced until they become routine.)

- Finally, teachers can have great discussions with students in whole-class settings about the impact of body language on listeners in pairs, groups, or larger audiences.

CHAPTER 34
HITTING THE RIGHT NOTES

At a social studies conference years ago, I waited outside the door to the classroom where I was shortly to present a concurrent session. The long hallway contained several more classrooms with presenters who, along with me, awaited the arrival of conference participants fresh out of the keynote session in the school's auditorium. No one had signed up in advance for any of the concurrent sessions, so well over 200 social studies teachers, armed with session titles and descriptions, descended on this one hallway.

MUSIC IS A MARVELOUS MOOD MODIFIER

I was standing in the hallway to the side of the classroom door, tapping my foot to "Sing a Song," by Earth, Wind, and Fire, which was emanating from my Bose SoundDock from inside the room. I had twenty-five chairs in the classroom, but we had more than fifty happy, toe-tapping participants who came to my session because it promised to be different. It was, and the difference began with Earth, Wind, and Fire.

Music is a mood lifter. Music makes us tap our toes, even if we aren't familiar with the tune or the lyrics. "The ability for songs to deliver an emotional lift," write Allen and Wood (2013), "is one of the main reasons

CHAPTER 34

that music is one of the constants of the modern human experience—why we spend our lives literally surrounded by music" (p. 24). Yet students in middle or high school inhabit one classroom after another that are often silent, passive places that could benefit from a mood lifter or two in the form of music.

When students enter your classroom, why not greet them with an upbeat, energizing song that succeeds in putting them in a better mood? When they leave your classroom, why not send them out the same way? I have seen students of every age groove—rather than trudge—into classrooms. I've watched as most of the kids give the teacher a high five as they make their way into the hallway. They do not look down and shuffle to the exit; they often move out to the beat of an upbeat piece of music.

Playing music in the classroom does not, as Allen and Wood affirm, replace teaching. I knew a teacher who simply let the radio play while students filled in the blanks on worksheets. We still need to teach, but music can bring energy into the classroom. Music is emotionally charged, and "when your brain detects an emotionally charged event, your amygdala," says Medina (2014), "releases the chemical dopamine into your system. Dopamine greatly aids memory and information processing" (p. 112). Students who entered my largely silent, same-old-same-old classroom environment during my early years as a teacher fully understood that each day was going to be just like the last, with little energy.

I'm not saying music is an absolutely indispensable component of the learning process. Some of the best teachers I have ever coached or observed used no music at all. Others listen to music on their way to school and while they are getting ready for the day in their classrooms, and that puts them in a great mood. There are plenty of times to use music (Civil War music was an important part of that age, and can be used by social studies teachers in their classrooms) and plenty of times not to use it (while students are taking a test).

The use of music has become an integral part of my presentations around the country. The key for its use is a system where you have control through the use of a remote. With that hand-held piece of technology, you can stand anywhere in the classroom and control the volume or start or stop the music instantaneously. Some teachers will control the music from the electronic whiteboard, with a playlist on the computer. The overuse of music will probably lessen its impact and value, but for a quick energy boost, nothing beats it.

Build a Better Classroom with Music

Music can be content-specific. For anyone who teaches history or literature, there are period pieces that can help students understand the period. For example, "The White Cliffs of Dover" and "A Nightingale Sang in Berkeley Square" are two songs from World War II that perfectly describe the loneliness and longing of couples separated by the English Channel or various oceans or other bodies of water from 1939 well into 1945, when World War II finally ended.

Here are a few more ways to use music in the classroom:

- As students enter at the beginning of the day or at the start of a class period or block
- As students leave the classroom
- For transitions from seatwork to standing pairs, trios, or quartets
- As a quick energy booster
- As a signal to clean up or line up

CHAPTER 35
AS YOU WERE

I did a wonderful four-year stint as the yearbook adviser at the junior high and middle school level. Staff photographers underwent a week-long training session in the summer, and they became quite good at helping to tell the story of one year at our school. Every double-page spread in the book contained copy (text), and photographs were all captioned. The idea is that forty years hence, a member of that senior class whose memory may be fading a bit can tell exactly what is going on in every picture in the yearbook. And the story of every sports team and club has been captured for all time.

When a yearbook photographer approaches a student or a group of students, she does not want them to face her and smile (or make googly eyes). The photographer wants to capture what is happening at the moment. She wants to record students in the act of shooting the ball, dancing at the prom, or working together on a project in Mrs. Peabody's science classroom. The photographer will often say, "As you were." This indicates the group should go back to what they were doing, which is something that the photograph will faithfully capture. The photographer is in the business of NOT interrupting what is happening on the field or in the classroom. He or she just captures the moment as it is.

The same should be true of a classroom teacher working the room while students engage individually or in groups on tasks or projects. Just as getting it right with a series of yearbook photos means photographers must explain "as you were" to their subjects, teachers will need to explain this to students. I have watched as teachers approach a group of students as if everyone has just won the championship; high fives all around, coupled with, "How are you today, Mr. Albright. Good to see you. Like

CHAPTER 35

your suit." Displays like this are too often superficial and they waste time. When I see this, it also tells me that the group was probably not deeply engaged in whatever it was they were supposed to be doing. They were perfectly happy to extend a warm greeting to Mr. Albright for the simple reason that not much was going on.

In highly interactive classrooms where students are used to collaborating and getting deeply engaged in the work, the teacher can glide up next to the group and do what great teachers do best. They observe and they listen. They want to hear what is going on, and they may ask a couple of pertinent and guiding questions: "How do you know you are making progress toward your goal?" This may set up the next question: "What is your next step?" A teacher's group-side visit may last only a minute before he or she moves on, but a great deal can be gleaned in that sixty seconds or so.

The key for the teacher is to keep moving while continuing to listen and ask useful questions. Those two questions from the previous paragraph help students as well. They are forced to think about their thinking. Where are they now, and how do they know they are making progress? How does all this tie in to their ultimate learning goal? Teachers can explain this upfront, before students begin working collaboratively. "When I approach you or your group, just keep working. No need to break your concentration simply to greet me."

Teachers who have built solid relationships with students know that they can approach the group and eavesdrop, then ask a few guiding questions related to the task at hand. "We can't demand that students form healthy relationships with their peers," assert Frey, Fisher, and Smith (2019), "if we don't ourselves demonstrate the value of respect and regard we hold for our own students. Students look to us for guidance in how in-school relationships should be formed" (p. 96). And when students build working relationships with their teammates,

The real test comes when I, as a classroom *visitor*, walk up next to a group of students working on a project or task. I, too, want to see what they are doing, and I may ask how they know where they are in the process. What they are doing is the most important thing, and I, as a visitor learn more when the work continues unabated, unless I have a question or two. The classroom may not be quiet—and should not be so—because students will need to talk things over, ask each other questions, raise a possible problem, and do any number of things in the best interests of the group. When I see this as an observer, I know I am in a classroom full of students who are deeply—and willingly—engaged in their own learning.

The key to success with any group of students working on a task is this: Do they clearly understand the learning target? Do they know where they are in relation to that target? What will they do next; what is the next step in the process? If the target is not clear, the group cannot function. If they have no earthly idea what to do next, they will often resort to idle chatter, or they will stay relatively quiet and look like good and substantial things are happening until the teacher is on the other side of the classroom. Then all bets are off. A group of eighth graders with nothing to do can be a recipe for shenanigans.

Building working relationships with students is not about high fives and having a great sense of humor, although great teachers may well greet students with a high five and display an ebullient disposition. Teacher/student relationships are strengthened when Eddie understands that Mrs. Cooper consistently conducts herself with his best interests in mind. Relationships are strengthened when teachers prove they can be trusted, and when they treat students with respect on a daily basis.

The great teachers I have known and observed over the years have at least one thing in common: Their students know that what they are doing is worthwhile, and they are granted a good deal of autonomy in order to do it. They have a choice as well, "and when we give students choices about their work, we are sharing autonomy and power with them. When students know they will be sharing their writing or their research findings with others, or if they will perform in front of an audience, we can tap into their desire for purpose, belonging, and significance" (Anderson, 2019, pp. 107–108). Teachers and visitors approaching such groups at work can observe, listen, ask questions, and then move on. As with a good yearbook photographer, what is happening will be recorded, remembered, and valued.

Build a Better Classroom by Effectively Working the Room

Great teachers work the room constantly, moving from desk to desk and group to group, and they do so with purpose and design. If students are

CHAPTER 35

working independently, teachers can hunker down next to a student and find out how that in-class writing assignment is going. As they circulate between individual students or groups, the idea is to do so without taking students off task. Now is not the time to chat about the basketball game last night.

- When working the room while students are engaged in tasks or more complicated projects, concentrate on listening, then asking thoughtful questions directly related to what they are doing, where they are now, and where they are going.

- Explain to your students that this is your object as you walk around. You may approach their desks or their groups on many occasions, but they should continue to work with each other, talk among themselves, and otherwise move toward whatever learning goal has been established for that task or project.

- You can use the example of a high school basketball coach who quietly observes a group of players involved in a scrimmage. What she eventually says is based on what she saw as they practiced. It is not a time for a general "rah-rah" moment; good feedback is specific and timely. Too many pieces of feedback given at once will most likely confuse players on the hardwood or students in the classroom. Again, *you can explain all this to your students*. Then follow through.

CHAPTER 36
BRINGING THEM BACK

One of the big little things that I notice in classrooms has to do with getting the attention of a classroom full of students. The teacher may have fifteen paired conversations going on for a couple of minutes, at which point she wants everyone's undivided attention. Or after a fire drill that completely disrupted whatever lesson was in progress, the teacher needs to shift gears to instruction mode. Or students are entering the classroom after lunch or recess. Teachers are constantly moving from one activity to another, or they are transitioning students from their seats to standing pairs or groups, and making this happen smoothly requires an auditory or visual cue that works—every time.

I have seen teachers become frustrated when unable to get the attention of their students. In one memorable instance many years ago, I watched as an eighth-grade teacher tried waving her arms as she said, "Okay, everyone, let me have your attention!" and "Class, let's calm down now!" or words to the like effect, to *no* effect. Finally, she quit talking and walked to the edge of the classroom next to the windows—and simply stopped talking. And that got her students' attention; *they were used to talking over her*. It was the teacher's silence that finally brought them back to her.

In Chapter 3, I emphasized the importance of establishing routines, then practicing them over and over until they contribute to the smooth running of classrooms at any level. At the top of the list at the end of that chapter was getting the attention of students, and the teacher I observed who was frustrated to the point where she gave up made the mistake of using one verbal cue after another, her voice rising in volume with each new attempt at getting her students to stop talking. Multiple cues, often created in the spur of the moment, don't work. In her book *Interactive Modeling* (2016), Margaret Berry Wilson encourages teachers to keep it simple: "Teachers who constantly change routines (or modify expectations each time) invite confusion and testing from students" (p. 52). That frustrated teacher's students were testing her, and because she had not established an expectation, backed by a practiced routine, her lesson plan for that class period went off the tracks.

I recently observed a second-grade teacher who taught her students visual cues for everything from asking to go to the restroom to giving her their undivided attention. I watched as she had them talk in pairs (seated on a rug) about a particular topic; when she put two fingers to her lips, the conversations died down as students finished their thoughts, thanked each other, and turned to face her. This took a few seconds. She told me she practiced several visual cues during the twenty-minute class meetings during the first days of school until they became routine. After a weeklong vacation, she said, she might have to practice a bit until they were back on track.

I have yet to meet a teacher who didn't agree that time is of the essence in classrooms, no matter the subject area or grade level. Frustration is the enemy, and a lack of expectations backed by practiced routines can lead to exasperated teachers and students. I am a fan, as every one of my books and presentations will attest, of highly interactive classroom environments. The only essential routine in a classroom filled with worksheets and teacher talk involves a sharpened pencil and the restroom pass. Students should be working and talking together in pairs and groups, and this means those classrooms can become intentionally noisy places. And that means the cue for bringing students back needs to be well established and effective.

Students who have several teachers may have several cues to which they must respond throughout the day. In some schools, basic routines like those connected with getting the attention of students are adopted school-wide, so that students don't experience confusion and frustration with a multiplicity of procedures.

Building a Better Classroom with a Single Cue for Bringing Students Back

Some students are more visually oriented, so that a raised hand catches their attention. Others may be more attuned to auditory cues. Teachers can cover the bases here by establishing one cue that combines the two preferences, visual and auditory. Here is one way to use that kind of cue:

Fourth graders have been in standing pairs for two minutes, pencils and notebooks in hand, as they write down a few questions they might have after viewing a short video on the water cycle. The teacher has been circulating and eavesdropping on students as they talk and write, and with the two minutes about to expire, she walks to the front of the room (the power position) and faces the students.

> **Direction 1:** The teacher raises both hands, *palms toward the students*, and says, "Please finish the question you are writing down." (Pause until it appears they are done.)
>
> **Direction 2:** With a sweeping gesture toward the students, she says, "Please thank your partner for sharing."
>
> **Direction 3:** With her palms now turned inward toward herself, she says, "Please turn and face me."

If the teacher wants to debrief at this point by having students share questions they wrote down with the class, she can do this. At any rate, her students know they need to wait until the next direction to return to their seats. She may want to get them back to their seats at this point, where they can share the questions generated in the standing pairs with their shoulder partners at their seats. In this case, Direction 3, following the thanking of their partners might be as follows:

> **Direction 4:** The teacher spreads her arms with palms out again, saying, "Please return to your seats."

Notice the use of the visual (palms outward, toward the students, then inward toward herself), in conjunction with the auditory. The gestures

CHAPTER 36

are congruent with the voice. So that this works properly every time, that teacher would have modeled, practiced, and revisited the cue when necessary. Winging it with multiple routines is likely to cause confusion and resentment on the part of students, along with mounting frustration on the part of the teacher. If time is indeed of the essence, then teachers should take the time to identify a single cue and do what is necessary to make it efficient and effective—every time.

CHAPTER 37
ONE-AT-A-TIME DIRECTIONS

The emphasis in chapter 36 was on the importance of not wasting time by experimenting with too many ways of getting the attention of a classroom full of students. This chapter deals with what teachers do once they initially *have* their attention. The next order of business is setting in motion a lesson or activity of some sort, and that requires a set of clear directions, delivered in a way that does not lead to confusion or waste valuable time or effort.

When I'm observing or coaching in a classroom, I watch the students and read their body language, which can, in fact, say a great deal. And I gauge their reactions to verbal directions given by their teachers. A few years ago, I watched as a sixth-grade teacher gave a set of at least five verbal directions to her students at the beginning of a class period. Then she turned them loose—and spent the next fifteen minutes trying to bring order to a chaotic situation. Of the thirty-plus students in that classroom, maybe a few heard and internalized those directions. The others were confused, and that confusion caused any number of disruptions from students who simply gave up and raised their hands, needing her attention and guidance.

When I first started presenting to teachers around the country, I sometimes gave too many verbal directions before an activity, at which point the questioning hands went up—but not before I had set the activity in motion. In other words, an otherwise effective activity was stopped after maybe fifteen seconds. I had short-circuited my own forward momentum, and that cost me time and credibility in the eyes of the session participants.

CHAPTER 37

Now I follow a very simple rule: Give verbal directions one at a time, then make certain everyone is on board before moving on. Take that first example of the teacher who gave multiple verbal directions, then spent precious time picking up the pieces. She would have been better off giving them one at a time, so that when the last direction was in place, every member of that large English class would have been ready to proceed.

Teachers are sometimes reluctant to put students into groups, and I always suggest teachers begin with pairs. Also, as a Press and Release mechanism (chapter 13), getting students up, moving, and in standing pairs can set the stage for a great paired conversation. However, and I have seen this happen many times, teachers will sometimes say, "Okay everyone, when I say go, stand and move around the room until you find a partner. Go!" This can be an invitation to chaos, especially if students have not done this before. Kids will wander aimlessly for a minute or so or look for a friend on the far side of the room—then choose to get there slowly. Multiple directions can create multiple problems.

Here are some simple one-at-a-time directions teachers can use to make sure that students get sorted quickly:

Direction 1: "When I say go, stand behind your chair and push it under the table. Go!" (Wait until everyone is in place with chairs pushed in. If even one student has not done what you have asked them to do *and you move on*, you have given permission to everyone to follow that student's lead next time. With each successive direction you give, more and more students will get the message that they need not comply in a timely fashion. Remember, *you* control the timing, and it is you who set the expectations—and insist they are met.)

ONE-AT-A-TIME DIRECTIONS

Direction 2: "Raise your right hand high in the air." (Wait until every right hand is up.)

Direction 3: "When I say go, with your hand held high, walk three or four steps in any direction and shake hands with a new partner. Go!" (By having their hands in the air, a clear indication that they all have partners is that there are no more hands in the air. If there is one hand left, it means there are an odd number of students in class that day. Instruct that student to make a trio with one of the pairs.)

Direction 4: "Standing next to your partner, turn and face me." (Wait until everyone is facing you.)

Now you are ready to proceed. Each student has a partner and is facing you next to that partner. Time to begin the activity. There is no need for them to know what you are going to do until the process-related part of getting into pairs is finished.

One-at-a-time directions save time and confusion. In a classroom filled with thirty students, confusion is not your friend—or theirs. Process first and content second.

Building a Better Classroom with One-at-a-Time Directions

My experience is that students don't really want a lot of chaos in the classroom, and giving one-at-a-time directions helps things run smoothly. Here are a few practical suggestions to make directions easier for students to digest:

- One science teacher in Texas took dozens of digital pictures of every lab setup she wanted students to construct during that semester. At the beginning of the lab, she simply projected the appropriate picture up on the screen mounted near the ceiling, then told them to get the lab set up. She didn't have to say anything; it was all there right in front of them. She gave them a set amount of time and turned them loose. Visual beats auditory every time.

- When giving verbal one-at-a-time directions, use eye contact to make sure everyone is in place, ready for the next direction. Learn to wait; the minute you give a direction before everyone is ready, you give your students permission to talk or dawdle every time.

- If students have to read something on the screen before they begin the activity, don't read it to them. With an open palm pointed in the direction of the screen, invite them to read the passage or chart. Read it silently to yourself, then look around to make sure they are done with it before proceeding.

- Finally, the time to practice those one-at-a-time directions, which will be used frequently, is during the first week of school. There doesn't even need to be an activity behind those process-related directions at that point. It is all about getting them used to getting into pairs quickly and efficiently. When a content-rich activity is introduced, the process is automatic.

CHAPTER 38
AVOID COMPETING WITH THE LAWNMOWER

For two years in the 1980s, I taught in a portable classroom. It leaked, as portables often do, and when the leaks were fixed, others took their place. I had a lot of buckets, as I recall. Also, the school was in the flight path of a major air base, so several times a day, fighter jets came and went, shook the building. And there was always the riding lawnmower. I didn't care for all the noise, for the simple reason that it interrupted my lectures. No doubt trains, planes, and automobiles were welcome by my seventh graders who had to listen—or pretend to listen—to my voice for much or most of the class period. I had chapters to cover, for heaven's sake!

Our brains play a big role in dealing with external stimuli like the lawnmower or a noisy HVAC system. Our RAS (Reticular Activating System) helps students "separate stimuli that are relevant from stimuli that are irrelevant" (Almarode and Miller, 2013, p. 69). It is when students are faced with the same-old-same-old classes filled with lecture or worksheets that the RAS stops working effectively, and outside stimuli capture and hold their interest. The teacher who spends much of every class talking, followed by a predictable bit of seatwork, is likely to find that students will have trouble staying on task. When students have to deal with a predictable and boring routine day in and day out, they are much more likely to be distracted by external stimuli, or by thoughts of the game on Friday night.

So why is it that I can walk into any number of classrooms as a visitor, as I did two years ago in California, and none of the students gave me a bit of notice? They were, you see, used to seeing visitors in that science classroom, and they were too busy and engaged to be distracted by

CHAPTER 38

them—or by anything else. I was encouraged by the administrators and teachers to ask questions of the students in every classroom I visited, and I did. They answered my questions politely, then returned to their projects without missing a beat. I'm guessing the riding lawnmower would have to pass through the center of that middle school classroom before those kids registered the unusual nature of the act.

In one fifth-grade classroom I observed years ago, students worked in groups on a writing assignment. The teacher often had them write independently in class as well, and the interpersonal skills developed in the groups carried over into independent work. Rather than rely on the teacher for feedback or ideas, students in that classroom could consult the anchor writing that was hanging from the ceiling and tacked to the wall. It seemed to me that the classroom was a virtual writing lab, complete with student "experts" who were consulted frequently by classmates. Serravallo (2021) stresses the value of the conversations that are taking place within the groups. "Within groups, they might overhear you giving feedback to a friend, which they can then apply to their work." All this amounts to "built-in support for learners" (p. 8). Classrooms like this one and the eighth-grade science classroom in the previous paragraph are sometimes noisy places, and this is as it should be. In both those classrooms, students had a high degree of agency, and they were truly engaged in working toward learning targets.

After observing and coaching in hundreds of classrooms, I've come to the following two conclusions: (1) If students are really invested in their own learning, no amount of potential distractions will take them off task, and (2) If they are not invested in their own learning, no amount of admonition on the part of an adult to "pay attention" is going to keep them on task. Students learn early on how to play the game; they can fake engagement with the appropriate body language and facial expressions, but they are not engaged. They are not invested in their own learning and won't accomplish much, if anything, but teachers can be fooled into believing there is much work going on in the classroom.

Boredom is the enemy in classrooms; if students go to a better place in their minds after a few minutes, the game is up as interest in the proceedings goes down. This can lead not only to glazed expressions but to misbehavior that is disruptive. As Hattie and Zierer (2018) point out,

"Classroom disturbances can usually be avoided when students experience the lesson as stimulating and interesting, as informative and fun" (p. 46). Students who are admonished frequently to "pay attention because this is on the test" are more likely than not to take an interest in the wall clock or the riding lawnmower in the courtyard.

A teacher who is talking for a long period of time simply cannot compete with extraneous noises or visual distractions inside or outside the classroom. Glaring at Eddie and saying, "Stay with me now!" will not help Eddie, and it will serve as an additional distraction to everyone else. But I have been in countless classrooms where the teacher can walk around the classroom asking goal-related questions of individual students or groups without distracting anyone. The students expect the questions, and they can confidently provide answers. And visitors don't bother anyone; they, too, are expected.

Build a Better Classroom by Involving Students in Their Own Learning in the Classroom

Every adult is a veteran student, and we can well remember, sometimes going back decades, in which classes we were meaningfully engaged for all or most of the class period or block. Three-hour night classes in college could be downright painful if my job was simply to listen to the professor drone on, taking a few notes, and watching the clock behind his or her head. A heavy snow falling outside the windows provided many a distraction on my Pennsylvania college campus. I suspect the reader can identify a few distractions, too, back in the day.

Lessons can be constructed so that students are frequently in pairs or small groups, working toward common learning targets. Teachers become facilitators of process as they ask questions while working the room. Some of the most effective teachers I have seen over many decades talk less and listen more. When in classrooms where students are well supplied with worksheet after worksheet, while the teacher grades papers at his or her desk, I watch as students quickly become disengaged, act out, daydream, clock-watch, or attend to an open book or a cell phone below desk level. Kids know time wasters when they experience them, and they act accordingly.

CHAPTER 38

Teachers have control over how they and their students spend their time in classrooms. Structuring lessons that are high in student engagement and low in teacher talk and busy work will most likely keep students interested and productive—and it ought to keep the lawnmower at bay.

CHAPTER 39
TEACH STUDENTS TO PARAPHRASE FOR UNDERSTANDING

The teachers who get the best out of their students when it comes to classroom conversations—academic and otherwise—have taken the time to have students practice active listening. Students learn the importance of body language on the part of the speaker *and* the listener. They learn to use appropriate eye contact and hand gestures, and they discover the benefits of trying to understand what their partner in a paired conversation is trying to say or explain. Students are nothing if not perceptive, and they know when someone to whom they are talking is truly trying to understand what they are trying to communicate.

The listener can certainly ask questions as a way of clarifying what the speaker just said, of course, and teachers can model this, as we'll see in chapter 43. In her book, *Demystifying Discussion* (2022), Jennifer Orr points out that making speedy assumptions about what another student says can lead to problems. (I would add from experience that this applies to adult conversations as well.) In addition to asking questions, the listener can paraphrase to clarify what the speaker has said. As Orr maintains, "Paraphrasing what you are hearing helps ensure that you understand—and it can also help the speaker because, upon hearing their thoughts paraphrased, they may realize they did not say what they intended to say" (p. 85).

For the listener, taking a breath and then paraphrasing is a great way not only to show that we understand what someone is telling us, but, according to Zwiers (2019), it allows the listener to:

CHAPTER 39

- keep track of what you are hearing,
- describe what the partner just said in your own words,
- check to see whether what you heard was the talker's intended message,
- organize the partner's points,
- help the partner and the conversation stick to the topic and build the intended idea, and
- chunk and highlight key information to make it more memorable (as we do in reading). (p. 54)

Learning to paraphrase is not a matter of "telling" students how to do it, then cutting them loose. Teachers need to model paraphrasing with another adult or with a student, then the students need to practice until they feel comfortable with it. I suggest teachers put students in standing pairs around the room so that other conversations don't serve as a distraction. Below are a few stems students can use when paraphrasing, courtesy of Art Costa (2008), and he suggests they not begin with the word "I." "The phrase 'What I hear you saying . . .' says Costa, "signals to many speakers that their thoughts no longer matter and that the paraphraser is now going to insert his or her own ideas into the conversation" (p. 135).

- You're suggesting . . .
- You're proposing . . .
- So, what you're wondering . . .
- So, you are thinking . . . (p. 135)

In an elementary Virginia classroom one morning, I watched as second graders stood, paired, and practiced paraphrasing for sixty seconds. Then the teacher used music to get them to their next partner, and they continued practicing. This whole activity went on for almost ten minutes, at which point the teacher debriefed with them, letting them share problems they might have been experiencing during that ten-minute activity. When the teacher and I met later in the day, I asked her how she prepared them for that smooth and seemingly effortless exercise. She said she spends time every day on paired discussions, working with her students on several listening skills. In short, these were disciplined students who knew what they were doing, and they had learned how to actively listen to their second-grade colleagues.

Build a Better Classroom by Teaching Students the Power of Paraphrasing

If we want students to support their classmates in conversations, they should practice paraphrasing over many days and weeks—*until it becomes second nature for them*. Paraphrasing can become a habit if, as with anything, it is used enough. The class full of second graders I watched practice their paraphrasing did very well, and they were proud of that. Practice is never going to make perfect, by the way; the pursuit of perfection is aspirational at best, but helping students get measurably better is entirely attainable.

Most importantly, perhaps, are the messages paraphrasing sends to the speaker from the listener. "An effective paraphrase expresses empathy by reflecting both the feelings and the content of the message," according to Art Costa (2008, p. 146) Those messages are:

a. I am listening to your ideas.

b. I understand your thinking.

c. I am trying to understand your thinking.

d. I care about your thinking. (Costa, p. 146)

A text on one's phone can be misinterpreted, and the sender of the message may not even be near enough to his or her phone to clear something up. Add to that the fact that words typed in text mode can be changed, as I have found to my dismay, and not taking the time to proof what was typed before hitting send can result in unintended negative consequences. But when two people are face-to-face in conversation, and when the listener demonstrates by his body language and his attempts to clear up any misunderstandings *in the moment*, the results can be far more

CHAPTER 39

satisfying for both parties. Paraphrasing is a great tool in the hands of someone who knows how to use it, and teachers can provide that tool, no matter the grade level or subject area. As with any tool, it is useless if it is never removed from the toolbox. And *this* tool is a big little thing of much value in classrooms—and, make no mistake, in life.

- Give students plenty of opportunities to meet and have basic, personal conversations in pairs before moving to more academic conversations.

- Find another adult and model paraphrasing with that person, with each of you taking turns as the listener. Or find a student you can coach to be your partner as you model paraphrasing.

- Walk around the room as they talk, listening and gauging how they are doing. As they get more comfortable with the process, you can move into more academically oriented conversations using paraphrasing.

CHAPTER 40
THE TWO-MINUTE DRILL

In chapter 27, I stressed the importance of making students feel welcome by greeting them with a smile and, perhaps, some upbeat music. A series of high fives and the sight of a teacher who is always in a good mood provide a great start to the day or to the class period. A teacher who sits behind their desk as students enter the room, grading papers or reading a memo from the office, does nothing to lift moods or provide a positive beginning to the next hour or block.

Working the room for teachers begins as students move down the hall and toward the classroom. Some teachers regularly spend a couple of minutes talking with a particular student or pair of students, perhaps congratulating them on their performance the evening before at the band concert or asking about an older brother and former student who had been in the news lately after having been involved in an accident. In an educational environment where time is of the essence, there can be no better use of time than building rapport with students, letting them know how much they are appreciated. "If you let them know that your interest in them goes beyond their names and a few interesting facts, they will begin to respond to you in positive ways," write Wyatt and White (2007), in Bluestein (2010, p. 169). By contrast, I have known teachers who don't take the time to learn the names for weeks or even months.

When teachers take the time to build relationships with students, they are modeling the skills those students can use to build their own solid student-to-student relationships. Because of the ever-looming tests, we tend to focus overmuch on course content, while ignoring social skills that help make the building of relationships possible. Examples of those social skills, says Zwiers (2020), "include being patient; forgiving others;

CHAPTER 40

sacrificing; valuing others' ideas; not making fun of others, wanting the best for your friends; trusting others; and being trustworthy, honest, loyal, empathetic, and nonjudgmental" (p. 40). Building a learning culture in any classroom is virtually impossible without focusing on the kinds of positive relationships that nurture that culture.

It has been my pleasure for the past seventeen years to observe and coach in scores of schools around the country, and I have found that simply walking through the halls of any elementary or secondary building tells me a great deal about the culture of the school. If, as I once observed, two teachers are arguing in the hallway, the modeling that is taking place is not conducive to building a school-wide culture of learning—or civility. In a high school setting, the time between classes is perhaps four or five minutes at most, and that is prime time for the building of teacher-student relationships. Standing in the hallway while talking with a group of teachers does nothing to further the development of relationships with those that matter most—the students.

In *The Passionate Teacher* (2001), Robert Fried references teachers new to the profession, but what he has to say about relationships applies to all teachers: "It's the *kids*. Teaching is about the kids. It's about *you* and the *kids*. Teaching is about you helping the kids to become powerful as learners. For you, a beginning teacher, nothing matters more than your relationships with your students. Nothing else even comes close" (p. 295). When I think about my own favorite K-12 teachers, the ones I appreciated the most were those who made it their business to get to build a solid personal and working relationship with me.

Interactions between teachers and students can be incredibly impactful, and "Words given by teachers have the potential to be remembered, either positively or negatively, for a lifetime" (Hattie and Clarke, 2019, p. 45). The teacher who loses his temper and dresses down a student in front of the class just made a huge withdrawal from the relationship bank. The use of sarcasm can also work to break down relationships. Denton (2015) reminds us that sarcasm is, by definition, insulting. A teacher might say to a student who just entered the room, "Glad you could join us today, Fred!" The students may laugh, and the teacher may think it is funny, but Fred doesn't, even if he smiles or laughs himself. "The position of the teacher may be diminished in the other students' eyes as well," says Denton, "even if they laughed, because they no longer see the teacher as an authority who protects their emotional safety but someone who freely uses the currency of insult" (p. 16). The teacher who loses his temper or thinks sarcasm is simply another form of humor is going to eventually find the going rough when it comes to building a community of learners. Social skills are essential in building such a community, and modeling those skills by every adult in the building is an absolute prerequisite.

Teachers, in their role as presenters, generally use two voice patterns in classrooms. The teacher's *credible* voice "is often associated with sending information or giving directions" (Zoller and Landry, 2010, p. 3). This is what high school students probably heard most of the time in my history classrooms; I was forever sending information (lecture) or giving directions (worksheets, tests, or quizzes). The *approachable* voice, and Zoller and Landry are referring specifically to professional presenters, "use this voice pattern when seeking information, posing questions, or asking participants to consider an idea" (p. 3). This also applies to classroom teachers, and the approachable voice is also used in the telling of stories and, of course, in sidebar conversations with students: "I wanted you to know, Sophie, that the orchestra concert last night was incredibly enjoyable, and your flute solo was excellent."

Part of the beauty of effective conversations, unlike lectures, is that both conversation partners can contribute. A fifth-grade teacher whom I observed on more than one occasion, Chuck Kenison, made it a habit to "hunker down" (his phrase) next to his students (so that he was at eye level with them) while they worked. He could provide feedback, ask questions related to the work at hand, or sometimes simply engage them in a casual conversation. Importantly, their body language told me they thoroughly enjoyed his visits. In this and in many other ways, Kenison built solid relationships with his students (Nash, 2014).

Building a Better Classroom with a Plethora of Two-Minute Drills

Over the years, I have seen teachers make effective use of what might be called the "two-minute drill" in their classrooms. The time between classes is the perfect opportunity for one or several short conversations with students, all aimed at building rapport and making students feel

CHAPTER 40

comfortable in that classroom. Those mini conversations allow teachers to reveal a bit about themselves as well. I discovered that one of my seventh graders, a trumpet player in the band, also had a love of jazz, and that formed the basis for many a conversation in the hallway or in the lunchroom. (All the teachers on our seventh-grade "Apple Team" ate in the cafeteria at lunch, not in the faculty lounge or in the faculty dining area. It was the perfect opportunity to chat a bit with students in the lunch line or when they were done eating.)

Here are a few social skills teachers can model with students during those short conversations:

Teachers can:

- take care not to dominate the conversation, pausing to allow the student listener to respond,

- ask questions that will open students up and allow them to share and expand upon ideas,

- shift from the credible voice (lecturing, for example) to a more approachable voice (used in adult conversations as well),

- steer clear of sarcasm or passing judgment on others,

- keep body language positive by not hovering over the student, crossing one's arms (which says to the listener that you are closed to what he or she is saying),

- and thank the student for taking the time to chat.

CHAPTER 41
CONNECTING WITH STORIES

How many of us can remember a teacher who used storytelling to inspire students and capture their interest in what otherwise might have been pretty sterile and uninspiring material? My favorite college professor, Dr. Joel Haines, made English history come alive with stories that took us back several centuries and captivated us in the process. His stories were much anticipated by his undergraduate and graduate students; his classes were full and stayed that way throughout the semester.

Dr. Haines understood the value and power of a good story in ways that a large majority of my teachers and professors did not. "The problem," assert Caine and Caine (1994), "is that a straight historical narrative often misses the power of a story because it tends to be presented as additional inert surface knowledge. Our experiences are dramatic. They include emotion, mystery, tension, and climaxes" (p. 122). In 1992, as a seventh-grade U.S. history teacher, I incorporated an experience from my past in my lessons.

When I was thirteen, growing up on the shores of Lake Erie, a friend and I were given a tour of his grandparents' basement, which contained a small, cramped room hidden by a wall of rocks that was not part of the home's structural foundation. That house, one of the oldest in my hometown, served as a station on the Underground Railroad in the decades before the Civil War. Runaway slaves would be hidden in the small room under the front porch until dark, when they would be taken a couple of miles down to the lake, then rowed out to a boat that would take them, under cover of darkness, to Canada and freedom. That (true) story provided a wonderful doorway into our study of abolitionism, and I

CHAPTER 41

sketched a drawing depicting the room, then listed the artifacts my friend and I discovered inside: checkers and a checkerboard, wooden plates and utensils, and a lantern. I asked them to talk with each other and figure out what the room might have been, providing even more clues as they talked.

Beginning with that hidden room and the artifacts it housed, I was able to ask my students what the purpose of the room might have been, what it must have been like for runaways to travel from the South all the way through Western Pennsylvania, much of it by foot and undercover of darkness, to the shores of Lake Erie and, eventually, to freedom. It was such a captivating a story that one of my students suggested we write a play that described the journey on the part of one runaway. And we did.

In their book on reading entitled *Comprehension: The Skill, Will, and Thrill of Reading* (2021), Fisher, Frey, and Law assert that "Storytellers can take action by acting out a skit, writing poetry, or conveying a personal narrative about a part of their own life" (p. 126). It was relatively late in my teaching career that I allowed myself to break out of lecture-and-note-taking mode to release the creative capacity of my students. Those seventh graders were immensely proud of the play they had created in my classroom, but I had to be flexible enough to let them put that creativity on display.

One of the finest fifth-grade teachers I have ever met had her students writing and acting out plays, singing, and otherwise tapping into their creative energies. That classroom was as close to a family as I have ever seen, and those well-developed relationships allowed the teacher to throw away the worksheets and the videos, and instead tap into a deep well of innovation and creativity. Oh, and the kids took care of the tests; they blew the lid off the Virginia standardized assessments at the end of the year. Take care of the kids, and they'll take care of the tests.

Kids have stories to tell and stories to write, and we as teachers can—and should—find ways to let them do that. It often brings them out of their shell, as it did with a special education student who gave—in front of my entire class—an incredible speech on abolitionism that literally brought the house down. Her classmates stood and cheered for her, as did I and my co-teacher.

Sometimes stories just break the ice when teachers are trying to get to know their students in September. Stories can, as we have seen, bring to life otherwise dry material. A story shared with a teacher while she hunkers down next to a student's desk can help build a relationship that had been lacking until the student quietly opened up. Stories have power; they convey emotion. They help us understand something we did not understand before. They make us feel better.

My grandmother read to me every night in my formative years. Every night before I went to bed, the stories she read conjured up images in my young brain, and they activated my imagination. Dozens of times over the years, I have watched as teachers in elementary school read to students arrayed on the floor on carpets. No video is necessary; their imaginations provide the images, as was the case with me at the age of three or four years old. When the storyteller speaks, we are with them. One teacher I knew years ago had a captain's chair, and when she went to the chair, her students sat back or forward, adjusting their bodies and their minds in anticipation of the story they knew was about to begin.

Build a Better Classroom with Storytelling

A master storyteller himself, Robert Garmston (2019), lists several reasons why stories have such a powerful influence on all of us:

> They teach, persuade, and enforce group beliefs and norms. They are uniquely effective because (1) they stimulate neurological changes that increase empathy; (2) they personalize presentation content, sending forth a gossamer filament that connects the audience and the presenter; (3) they open windows to the intuitive knowledge of an audience; and (4) they can tap the resources of the unconscious mind. (p. 5)

CHAPTER 41

Storytelling is a powerful tool in the hands of a teacher willing to sharpen his or her storytelling skills.

- Consider finding a captain's chair or a high stool that you use only when you tell a story. With elementary teachers, this may be a rocking chair. Going to that chair or stool signals that a story is coming.

- Remember that students have stories to share, too. A middle school social studies teacher working on an immigration unit in a community full of military families asked students to tell stories related to having to pick up and move from one neighborhood, city, or town to another. Turns out they had much in common with immigrants who had to leave friends, schools, and extended family members because of a necessary and often painful relocation.

- Your personal stories make you more human in your students' eyes, and those stories can often be used to highlight a point related to a particular unit of study.

- Stories can open the door to content in the way Dr. Haines, my favorite history professor, did on countless occasions.

CHAPTER 42
GETTING BETTER AT GETTING BETTER

We are shaped to a great extent by our past experiences, and as teachers, this is true when it comes to assessment. I can't speak for the reader, of course, but the kinds of feedback we tended to receive in school were more summative than formative. A letter grade on a test was pretty much the last word, unless the teacher had written, "You could do much better, Ronnie!" as a sort of assessment postmortem. I would not have known how to reply to this, except to say that I preferred to be called Ron. It was well intended on the part of the teacher, of course, and maybe she did believe that I could "do better" on the next test, but those kinds of comments didn't usually cause me to "put my nose to the grindstone" as we careened into chapter 15.

As I understood the game back in high school, we as students were in some sort of race to the top, in pursuit of the ultimate prize: salutatorian or valedictorian. My view of the summit was not quite in focus throughout my stay in the hallowed halls of our junior/senior high school, but even the student who ascended to the salutatorian step on the awards podium may have felt a failure, having fallen a fraction of a point behind the winner. It was, as it had always been, of course, about the numbers.

White (2017) says she hears the desire of students "to have their work be valued or assigned a number because this is what they think school is about—that this number is the only thing that matters in the end" (p. xix). And when a teacher hands back test papers from the highest grade to the lowest in an attempt to light an academic

CHAPTER 42

fire under the "low performers" in the class (as more than one of my teachers did), students can be forgiven if they think the only thing that matters is the grade.

I don't pretend to be an expert on assessment, but I do know this: Students who are working on a particular piece of writing at any level will benefit from feedback given *while the work is in process*, with the goal of making *that* essay, paragraph, or term paper better. While some few students may respond to the clarion call of competition, most students, in my experience, won't. I did respond to immediate and timely feedback, provided at intervals on the way to the finished product. "The greatest motivational benefits [of feedback]," write Hattie and Clarke (2019), "will come from focusing feedback on:

- the qualities of the child's work, and not on comparison with other children,
- specific ways in which the child's work could be improved,
- improvements that the child has made compared to his or her earlier work" (p. 4).

Providing feedback isn't about the attainment of perfection. It is about getting better at something. As students pick up multiple skills along the way, it's about getting better at getting better because learned skills are tools that can be used forever.

In *Classroom Assessment Essentials* (2024), Susan Brookhart encourages teachers to provide plenty of opportunities for peer feedback, provided a climate of learning is created in the classroom. Teachers should also "share learning targets or goals and criteria with students in a form they can use," then "teach students how to apply criteria to their own or others' work." Brookhart also says teachers should "make it fun. Student self- or peer assessment should result in feelings of self-improvement and the satisfaction of working together on something important" (p. 48). Unfortunately, because I was in compliance-and-control mode in all but the last year of my years of teaching, my emphasis was on "Do your own work!" That was followed by filling in the little squares in the indispensable grade book.

174

Build a Better Classroom with Plenty of Assessment-Related Questions

I always encourage teachers to "work the room" as students work on projects individually or in groups. I have observed many teachers who move from student to student or group to group, asking questions that provide information for the teacher and help students focus as they move toward project-specific learning targets and overall instructional goals.

There are assessment questions, writes White (2019), that "teachers may be trying to answer to formatively assess students' work and conversation starters that will provide formative assessment during extended exploration" (p. 100). The first set of questions, a few of which I have listed below, are those that teachers might ask themselves before beginning conversations with individual students:

- How is this student progressing in relation to the target, outcome, or goal?
- Who is helping the learner and how?
- How might I help this learner?
- How might I offer feedback?
- How might we set a goal together?
- How might I help the student understand the criteria for success?

The second set of questions, affirms White, can serve as conversation starters as the teacher works the room:

- What have you done so far?
- What is working?
- What isn't working?
- Where have you felt challenged? What did you do about it? Did it help?

CHAPTER 42

- Where are you going next? How might you get there?
- What are you still wondering?
- How will you know when you are successful?

This last set of questions each serves to get students thinking about where they are, where they are going, what they need, and so forth. If a student is having problems with grammar, that should come up, and the teacher can provide some feedback. If the learning targets are not clear, this conversation can serve as an opportunity to rectify that.

This certainly beats the question I used to ask regularly as the students worked on an in-class assignment: "Does anyone have questions?" or "Is anyone confused?" I might as well have asked, "Who is willing to describe publicly your state of confusion or admit to your lack of understanding? Anyone? No? Good! Keep working."

I often asked the ever-popular question, "Who needs help?"

Thinking back on it, I think *I* did.

CHAPTER 43
TOLERATE AMBIGUITY AND ENCOURAGE QUESTIONS

As a sales manager for a major yearbook company in the early 1980s, I had occasion to interview scores of potential candidates for sales positions. I soon began to realize that the people I really wanted to hire were those who had good questions for me during the course of the interview. Good questions led to great conversations that highlighted a healthy curiosity on the part of those candidates; I learned much about them, and they learned a good deal about me and the company I represented. Because excellent questions are part and parcel of the repertoire of a good sales representative, candidates who sought clarity by asking lots of questions rose to the top when it came to hiring decisions. People—adults or students—who are not afraid to ask questions are those who will likely move closer to clarification and understanding of the topic at hand or of new ideas that have been brought up during a presentation or discussion.

Jeff Zwiers (2020) reminds us how important student-generated questions are in the learning process. When teachers or students are in presentation mode, time should be provided for students to ask the kinds of questions that provide clarity to themselves and others, and to provide support to the presenter. (p. 20) As students take notes, writes Zwiers, "Have students write down a number of clarify or support questions in their notes; they must ask one orally (in pairs or to the presenter) during the presentation" (p. 79). The key here is to create a situation where students are required to write—and then share—questions that provide clarity for the whole class, in all likelihood, and visible support for the presenter.

CHAPTER 43

What is even more powerful is when students can ask those clarifying questions in a small-group setting. I once heard a fifth grader say to the other members of her four-person team, after they had all reported on the research they had conducted the previous evening, "So what does this all tell us?" That is an incredibly thoughtful guiding question, and it was asked not by the teacher, but by a student team leader. It was no surprise to me that the teacher in that classroom had spent a good deal of time working with those fifth graders on the asking of those kinds of questions, and as I walked around the room listening to various groups, it was evident that she had succeeded.

Getting students to ask questions after reading something or listening to a short bit of lecture is often difficult. I call this Death Valley; the teacher says, "Does anyone have a question about what we just read?" The result is often silence and blank looks, as everyone waits for one person to break the silence with a question. In chapter 17 on priming, I suggested pairing the students up and having them share questions they might like to ask with that one partner. Then ask if anyone would like to share the question with the whole class. This gives students a chance to reflect a bit as they talk with another student, and it makes them more confident when asked to share later on. (This works with adults, too, and I use priming all the time in workshops.)

PART OF TEACHING IS HELPING STUDENTS LEARN HOW TO TOLERATE AMBIGUITY, CONSIDER POSSIBILITIES, AND ASK QUESTIONS.

One problem is that teachers, and I did this constantly as a young and wet-behind-the-ears beginner, ask for questions as a sort of throwaway line. Someone told them to "check for understanding" periodically, so "Does everyone understand?" or "Does anyone have questions?" are thrown out there in what amounts to a cue to students that it is time to move on, not time to reflect on—and ask good questions about—the material.

TOLERATE AMBIGUITY AND ENCOURAGE QUESTIONS

Teachers often spend too much time telling and not enough time asking questions to truly discover the depth of student understanding. Hattie and Clarke (2019) suggest that once students are involved in individual or group work in classrooms, teachers should be constantly on the move, asking probing questions like the following:

- Tell me/show me what you have learnt so far.
- Why do you think . . .?
- How could you change this to make it clearer? (p. 92)

I have seen teachers move about the classroom asking questions as they go, probing, seeking clarification, and checking for understanding on the part of students working in groups or individually. Feedback is a two-way street, and these questions and conversations can provide teachers *and* students with valuable input that will assist in the continuous improvement process. Teachers who put students to work, then sit behind the teacher's desk to grade papers, are missing out on dozens of opportunities to receive and impart essential feedback—and build relationships in the bargain.

We want students to build working relationships with peers, too. They need to understand how to communicate successfully with one another in pairs and groups, and this includes training them on ways to ask—and handle—questions. Students sometimes have a tendency to bristle when a partner asks a question, no matter how benign. I always suggest teachers begin the year by having students work in pairs and work on listening skills, something that takes time. "Listening is a lot of mental work, especially when, in pairs, you have to listen to every one of your partner's turns in a conversation" (Zwiers, 2019, p. 16). The only way for students to get used to talking, listening, and asking questions in pairs or groups is to practice on a regular basis. As students become used to taking part in classroom conversations, and if teachers are modeling good questioning techniques, they will learn to trust the teacher and each other when interacting face-to-face.

Classrooms should be places free of the fear of being wrong or lacking knowledge about something. Building strong teacher-to-student and student-to-student relationships is important for providing the foundation for a fear and tension-free classroom setting. In *Visible Learning: The*

CHAPTER 43

Sequel (2023), John Hattie points out that "The reason for developing positive relations is so that the class is an inviting place to come and learn, *errors and not knowing are welcomed as opportunities to learn,* and students can feel safe that they are fairly treated by all" (p. 202; emphasis mine). And for students who have had dozens or scores of teachers over the years, this isn't their first rodeo. "Students are great detectives of messages that indicate they are not welcomed," and that "they are not going to be treated fairly" (p. 203). Teachers who realize they teach people, not content, can create a community of learners where trust, respect, and a sense of acceptance provide a foundation for risk-taking and continuous improvement.

Build a Better Classroom by Encouraging—and Using—Good Questions

Here are some things to consider when planning lessons in any subject area:

- Make it a point to model good, thoughtful questions in your classroom.

- When students are working in groups or individually, use that time to hunker down next to them and ask questions that will help you understand where they are in their thinking.

- While on these walkabouts, help them clarify their goals or targets. What is the first thing they will do to get started?

- Work with students on listening skills that include paraphrasing and asking questions as ways of clarifying and deepening understanding.

- Emphasize the importance of body language and the role listeners have in keeping the conversation going: nodding the head slightly, staying focused, using eye contact when appropriate, and not being afraid to ask for a point of clarification when one's partner is done talking.

TOLERATE AMBIGUITY AND ENCOURAGE QUESTIONS

- Make it clear that it is perfectly acceptable to admit if one doesn't have an answer, an opinion, or an explanation. As the year progresses and trust and respect are the order of the day every day, my experience is that students will contribute orally to the lesson.

- Teachers can admit when they don't know something or have an answer. "I really don't have an answer to your question. How might we find the answer?"

This brings me to my final point on the asking of questions, no matter who generates them. A classroom climate devoid of trust will also be devoid of the basic curiosity that brings questions to the surface. Students must know that in this classroom *it is okay not to know something*; it is okay to ask a question without negative reactions on the part of classmates or the teacher. Building that kind of trust begins on the first day of school, and it must be reinforced throughout the school year. Students should not be afraid to share information or ask questions.

CHAPTER 44
HARNESS THE POWER OF NOVELTY

Rich Allen (2008) defines novelty this way: "When something is novel—new, different, or unusual—it stands out compared to what we've experienced previously or what we're expecting currently. That which is special or unique fascinates us, makes us curious, and draws our full attention toward it. If it is novel, we are captivated" (p. 64). An example of this would be when a teacher, for the first time, has his students stand, then move to find a partner in preparation for a standing-pair conversations. (As we saw in chapter 37, however, one-at-a-time directions will facilitate this transition better than simply saying, "Stand and find a partner.") For middle or high school students in particular, paired discussions, standing or otherwise, may truly be a novel experience.

Allen (2008) points out that when novel strategies are used many times, they become ritual in nature; the novelty wears off. In the case of paired discussion partners, Allen has some suggestions:

> Perhaps one day the teacher adds novelty into the ritual by asking students to decide who is "A" and who is "B." Then the teacher announces that B will go first—because B stands for "before." For novelty, this will work well a few times. However, now students will be expecting B to go first. When they come to expect this, the teacher might reverse things and announce that A will go first. When switching A and B is no longer interesting, the teacher can maintain novelty by announcing that the first person will be "whoever has the longest hair" or "whoever is wearing the brightest clothing." Again, this maintains the *ritual* of working with a partner while continually introducing novelty. (p. 81)

CHAPTER 44

It wasn't until my last year of teaching, before going to central office, that I began to experiment with novelty as a tool with which to spark interest and keep students actively engaged in the course material. During a lesson on slavery and the Underground Railroad, one of the seventh graders in my sixth period class raised her hand and asked, "Why don't we write a play about a runaway slave?" Keep in mind that most of my career had been spent in compliance-and-control mode, with an overhead projector always at the ready. In the face of this question, I threw caution—and my overhead marker—to the wind and replied, "Why not?" What resulted was the most powerful—and impactful—lesson of my classroom career.

I divided the class into five small groups, with each group responsible for one of five acts of a play we entitled *Toby*, after the name we gave our fictional runaway slave. In those days (early 1990s), the school library—and not the internet—was our most accessible and reliable resource (along with a great librarian), and those seventh graders went at that project with a will. The kinds of questions I got were surfaced by what they had *discovered*, and what they *wondered*, and not as a result of my usual post-lecture query: "Does anyone have any questions? No? Let's move on!" It took a week or so, but I can still remember handing each of them a copy of the play when it was edited and copied. (I regret that I no longer have my copy.) The energy and commitment of those middle school students taught me an important lesson, and I carried that lesson into my new position as social studies coordinator for fifteen middle schools.

In *Developing Growth Mindsets* (2020), Wilson and Conyers emphasize the importance of novelty in classrooms when it comes to developing brain connections: "Keep students' learning experiences fresh. Adding variety to lessons, group learning events, presentations, and assessments helps keep the brain engaged" (p. 40). I was present in a fifth-grade math classroom as the teacher had her students stand in the middle of a quiz while she played something called The Chicken Dance, and her students danced until the song was over. They then sat down and completed the quiz. She had a 1-100 number grid painted on the classroom floor, which is where her students reinforced their math skills while moving around the grid. She understood the power of novelty in her instruction, and her students appreciated it. So did I, as I got to do the Chicken Dance that day.

Building a Better Classroom with Novelty

I once had a teacher tell me that she had been teaching a couple of decades, and she had never been inside another teacher's classroom. She said this after I suggested she might want to observe other teachers in the building in order to get some ideas she could use in her classroom. Schools are filled with teachers who use novelty consistently in their lessons, and administrators who are in all those classrooms can—and should—make it possible for teachers to observe their colleagues in action.

Allen (2008) lists some key points in favor of incorporating plenty of novelty into lessons, and I have listed a few here:

- Novelty captivates our attention and sparks our curiosity.
- Novelty helps recall—we remember things that are unique.
- Novelty reduces external distractions and focuses students' conscious attention on the current lesson.
- Introducing new topics with novelty creates a high level of student engagement. (p. 81)

Having observed literally hundreds of teachers at all grade levels, I can attest to the positive effect of novel approaches to instruction. In largely teacher-centered classrooms, where lecture is king, as it was during most of my own teaching career, just getting students up, moving, and talking serves to increase their oxygen intake, even as it releases neurotransmitters like dopamine, which allows students to focus. In *ADHD 2.0* (2021), Hallowell and Ratey highlight the effects of the release of dopamine in the human brain.

> An increase in dopamine helps our nerve cells pass on information more "cleanly" from one to another. It helps to reduce the noise, quiet the chatterbox, and tune your brain to the right channel. If the signals aren't clear, it's easy to fall into confusion and anxiety. (p. 113)

Most teachers have students in their classrooms who have been identified as having ADHD, and many teachers are, in fact, ADHD. I had many such students, and my way of dealing with the issue was to tell them to

CHAPTER 44

"pay attention," since, I thought, they had an attention deficit disorder. I lectured constantly, and it never occurred to me that my students, ADHD or otherwise, might benefit from a bit of disruption in my ritualistic approach to teaching. I wasn't, as it turns out, paying attention. That is, until one of my seventh graders asked if they could write a play.

- Is there room in your lesson plan for something totally novel?

- Are there teachers with ADHD students who have tried novel approaches to reading assignments, quizzes, student presentations, or anything else? If so, can you observe those teachers?

- Would an ad hoc study group on the topic of novelty in the classroom be able to do a bit of research, sharing, and reporting out in blog form for the whole staff? (This could include the beneficial effects of novelty as it relates to memory and learning in general, not to mention raising the interest level of all students, not just those with ADHD.)

CHAPTER 45
PHYSICAL AND MENTAL STATE CHANGES

As a new teacher, I was fond of talking. I could rattle on about the Great Depression until, well, until my students began to show signs of depression. I thought talking was teaching, and on occasions when I suspected minds might be wandering, I used my command voice to bring everyone back: "Pay attention, now! This will be on the test!" I can't speak for biology or math teachers, certainly, but history teachers have a lot to say. Every year adds another chapter to an already heavy textbook.

Had I spent even a minute or so thinking back on my high school career or my college classes, it might have occurred to me that my attention span, even in subject areas that held my interest, was probably about fifteen minutes. Then the wooden restroom pass beckoned, or a trip to the pencil sharpener provided a way to get the blood flowing again. Rich Allen (2002) points out that students may get *something* from a fifty-minute class period, but

> Most important is the fact that, as time continues, learners will have to work harder and harder to stay focused on the information. Eventually a breaking point crash in on them. Reaching this point is readily apparent on learners' faces as they fall back on the skills all of us learned as teenagers: stare at the teacher, occasionally nod the head to send message of interest while our brain spaces out by thinking about anything but what is being taught at the moment. (p. 31)

Students who have been at the game a long time know how to play it; they can appear to be interested; in reality, of course, they have checked out and gone elsewhere in their minds.

CHAPTER 45

Neither their physical or mental state is conducive to accepting new information, and at some point the teacher may be the only one in the room who is engaged in any meaningful way.

In chapter 13 (Press and Release), we saw that when students have been taking notes for a large chunk of time, allowing them to pair up and take part in a Think-Pair-Share (TPS) activity that allows them to discuss the information they have in their notebooks with classmates, and by doing so doing get the benefit of different perspectives. It may also be that one conversation partner heard something the other missed. A TPS activity qualifies as a physical and mental state change.

When I started my teaching career in 1972, most classes at the secondary level were forty-five to sixty minutes in length. Now, of course, ninety-minute blocks proliferate in high school. I was working in central office when this transition was taking place, and it created problems for teachers who had become accustomed to the shorter class periods at the secondary level. To the extent that many teachers simply retained the same lecture format in the block, physical and mental state changes became more important.

There are many ways teachers can change the physical and mental state of students during the day, and I have taken these examples from notes I have taken over the years:

- One fourth-grade teacher had her students stand and discuss the short video on the water cycle they had just seen.

- A third-grade teacher played a bit of upbeat music, which was the cue for her students to move to the four corners of the room to pick up their handouts for the next activity.

- A fifth-grade teacher had her students stand and do a few in-place exercises.

- An elementary teacher had her students stand and face the electronic smart board, on which she projected a video of several of the teachers in that school in the gym, doing exercises to music. The students joined in, laughing all the way at their teachers in the video.

- A teacher had her fifth graders move around the room, solving math problems in pairs at stations, some of which were on the floor.

- A kindergarten teacher brought her students to the rug in front of her rocking chair, in anticipation of a bit of storytelling. The students were captivated by this teacher, who was a master storyteller.

Build Better Classrooms with Built-In State Changes

It is a pleasure to see teachers provide physical and mental state changes for students whose attention span is short. There are also classrooms where teachers understand the power of agency on the part of students, something described by Frey, Fisher, and Smith (2019) as "a person's capacity to take action and shape his or her destiny" (p. 21). Students can thrive if they are granted enough independence to make their own decisions and harness the power of collaboration with their classmates as they work toward learning targets and overall instructional goals.

"Teachers cannot *give* learners power; instead, they can create conditions within which learners can witness their own power and exercise it" (France, 2023, p. 55). When students collaborate in pairs or groups, and when they are free to move about the room to ask questions and seek feedback from classmates, work collaboratively instead of competitively, doing a bit of research on their iPads and moving about the room to accomplish all this—physical and mental state changes are built in. And, as one high school science teacher admitted to me twenty years ago, she finally understood she was not the only teacher in the room.

When students are deeply involved in collaborative learning projects, and when they can move about the room freely in search of feedback, answers, opinions, new ideas, corroboration, and someone with whom to share, the teacher needn't create state-change mechanisms or opportunities. They are already present and under the control of student learners.

- What can you do to change the physical and mental state of your students?
- Can you make time to observe teachers who regularly incorporate lots of state changes?

CHAPTER 45

- If you introduce more state changes into your routine, could you get feedback from your students as to how effective those changes were in their estimation?

- In looking at your lesson plan for tomorrow, are there two or three or more opportunities for movement, a Think-Pair-Share, a short period of in-place stretching or exercises?

CHAPTER 46
AVOID THE BLAME GAME

Every mystery story reveals someone who "dunnit." Once the reader discovers his or her identity, all that is left in the book are the acknowledgments. The culprit gets the blame and a long stay in the slammer. Things in the fictional community affected by the crime go back to normal, and all is well until someone else disturbs the status quo.

When I taught ninth-grade U.S. history and my test scores were as low as the energy level of my students, my colleagues helped me realize why that was so. The culprit, they insisted, was a textbook that was a couple of grade levels above my freshmen in terms of the reading level. Nothing I could do about that, I was told. Not my fault, I was told. Which was true, actually; I had not chosen the textbook. But it was the textbook I had been given, and the expectation was that I would use it in the time-honored tradition of assigning a section of several pages each night, along with the questions at the end of the section. The status quo is, as I have often said, a hard taskmaster.

The point here is that I let something I could not control stop me from trying something else, something new. I could have changed the way I taught; I could have used the textbook as a valuable resource; I could have innovated in ways that benefited my freshmen. But it was easier to continue as before, to teach in the way I had been taught in high school and college. After all, I had the culprit and my students had their marching orders.

We often resort to the finding of scapegoats when we find we are not successful at something others are counting on us to accomplish. "We fight these feelings of powerlessness," says Bailey (2014), "by starting a blame game whereby teachers blame parents, parents blame school

CHAPTER 46

systems and everyone, when exhausted, blames the children." We can blame a textbook for being too difficult; we can blame the administrators for being too lenient; we can blame students for not being like we were when *we* were in school—that is, students who *enjoyed* a good thirty-minute lecture. "In actuality," writes Bailey, "the blame game begins and ends with each of us" (p. 199). We can accept the occasional failure and do something about it, or throw in the towel.

The blame game is something everyone can recognize; it is played in every community, every organization, and every family. Instead of fixing the system, we find someone to blame for our problems. If we can fix blame, we are absolved from any further action on our own. If what is to blame is beyond our control, this offers us an easy out. The act of complaining or blaming others saps our energy, and those who spend their time in Negative Land sap our energy, too, if we let them, *but not letting them is a choice we make*. Speaking to building administrators, Schmidt (2002) says, "Sappers are not the people on your staff who drive you crazy. Sappers are the unconscious beliefs you reinforce with a negative monologue that runs through your head all day long. The voice of the sapper nags, criticizes, terrorizes, at a pitch so etheric that only dogs and your psyche can hear" (p. 30). The staff of a school that puts children first will likely not contain people who insist on sapping the energy and sanity of everyone; *principals* who put children first will likely, not to put too fine a point on it, send them packing.

Frankly, the best, most effective teachers I have met over the years are too busy to play the blame game. They have too much to do as they work to get better at getting better. They understand that doing the same thing over and over again gets the teacher and her students the same results, so they are quick to move outside their comfort zones into a place that brings more risk, but brings more reward. Risk may bring failure. It certainly breeds mistakes, but it is *outside our comfort zones* where we learn. It is because of our mistakes that we move forward. Every athletic coach knows that failure is an opportunity for growth. The blame game is a recipe for stagnation; it brings things to a halt.

We can sit down when faced with things we can't control that impact us on a daily basis, or we can find ways to get the job done regardless. "Most of us have a lot more power than we realize," write Silver, Berckemeyer, and Baenen (2015), and all of us can choose how we will react to those things we cannot control. We can throw up our hands and say, "I can't do this," or we can look challenge in the eye and say, "Well, okay then, I'll try it another way." (p. 10)

Progress is made in all those other ways, by teachers and administrators unwilling to get mired in the blame game that is often prevalent in faculty lounges and in faculty meetings.

Optimists, according to Aguilar (2018), are "neither naïve nor idealistic," and act in the following ways: Optimists don't play the blame game. They search for root causes for problems and challenges, and they "see opportunity in adversity." And they avoid the people I call the negaholics; when invited to a party, you bring the cheese and they bring the whine. Great teachers don't get sidelined by things outside their control; they concentrate on those things they can influence and control.

Build a Better Classroom with a Can-Do Outlook

I stopped going to the faculty lounge in one school where I taught; the negativity (and the smoke, to be honest) drove me away. (One principal told me she simply got rid of the faculty lounge.) Find colleagues who are more positive and innovative; you will learn much more from them, and you will develop your own social capital if you collaborate with them regularly.

Students encounter negativity, too, and sometimes it is from teachers who *choose* to be negative in their classrooms. Give your students a positive and safe place where they can take risks, make mistakes, fail forward, and smile and laugh right along with you. Involve your students in a discussion (in pairs at first, then in a whole-class setting) about how mistakes and failure can affect learning, and what we can do to turn them to our advantage. Offer stories of your own (professional or personal) that demonstrate how unforced errors or failing at something initially can serve as a springboard to ultimate success.

Nothing is gained by blaming anyone. Problems exist, to be sure. But "Problems deserve solutions, not scapegoats. Any program of continuous improvement will wither in the face of the blame game"

CHAPTER 46

(Nash, 2011, p. 39). Lee Jenkins (2003) urges teachers and administrators to avoid trying to blame others for problems and poor performance in the schoolhouse and the school district: "If blame could improve schooling, American K-12 education would be the envy of the world" (p. xxv). No doubt.

CHAPTER 47
THOSE TOO BUSY TO COMPLAIN

"There are many reasons teachers stop acting in the best interests of their students," write Silver and Berckenmeyer (2023). "Some are valid, but none are acceptable" (p. 53). In conferencing with hundreds of teachers over the course of many years now, there is one attribute that stands out among the most successful teachers with whom I have met: They long ago stopped listening to people who said something wouldn't work. Instead, they keep trying things they hope might work for the simple and compelling reason that *kids want teachers who are willing to take risks on their behalf.* In short, they preferred action to inaction. One teacher told me she wasn't about to try anything new; she was a couple of years from retirement, and apparently was watching the clock along with her students. Silver and Berckenmeyer (2023) warn us of the results of inaction:

> No matter what the cause, inaction can lead to fatalism, complacency, inattention, negativity, pessimism, isolationism, and boredom. Inaction is a clear signal that the person is no longer willing to take a risk or learn anything new. If we don't act, we fail by default and can't even learn from the experience. (p. 53)

Inactivity in classrooms tends to turn the occupants into clock watchers, and that includes a teacher I knew who read the newspaper while students completed worksheets.

The taking of risks always involves the making of mistakes, and it is how one deals with mistakes that determines whether or not they will remain in the game and continue to step up to the plate. Teachers who let

CHAPTER 47

the possibility of failure hold them back are making a choice; mistakes and failure are inevitable, but the way in which we deal with them is not. A baseball player who consistently gets one hit in three at bats is considered a great hitter. The fear of making mistakes has more negative power than the mistakes themselves.

The best teachers I have met over several decades are those who are not afraid to try something that takes them out of their comfort zones, when doing so might lead to failure. One teacher told me she had basically been doing the same thing in her classes for the better part of twenty-five years. Taking risks for her wasn't an option; yet taking risks—with the attendant possibility of failure—is the only way we can truly improve at anything. "At the level of the brain," writes Matthew Syed (2015), "the individual, the organization and the system, failure is a means—sometimes the only means—of learning, progressing, and becoming more creative" (p. 266). Teachers who constantly look for ways to improve how they do what they do, I have found, are too busy to complain about pretty much anything; they are incredibly and consistently positive, and don't have time for the negaholics in the faculty lounge. They attempt something new, reflect on it, and reject it out of hand or make changes—but they are always in motion.

For teachers who want to become better at what they do, self-reflection is a prerequisite. I once served under a deputy superintendent who abhorred meetings as information dumps; instead, we instructional coordinators used the meetings we had to think about, talk about, and otherwise reflect on the things we were doing on behalf of teachers in the district. Continuous improvement in any profession is not possible without self-reflection and self-evaluation. In fact, write Hall and Simeral (2015), "to be good at anything, you need to be thoughtful, intentional, and reflective about your practice" (p. 21). This takes time, of course, along with a willingness to look at things from the point of view of one's students.

A ruthless and student-led examination of teaching practices would necessarily send many a worksheet to the trash heap of forgotten things. Looking at lecture through their eyes—and ears—would lead to less of it. Trying new things will result in mistakes and occasional failures, but great companies and great teachers have something in common. Innovation entails risk, but iteration 2.1 is already on the drawing board, waiting for its debut.

Building a Better Classroom by Taking Risks on Behalf of Kids

I recently saw a request on social media from a teacher who wanted to hear from anyone using a particular strategy in math. Chances are, what you are thinking of doing has been done before, and social media makes it possible to find someone who has gone where you have not gone before. Requests at the building or district level using email or posting on an electronic message board might bring results as well.

If you find something you want to try, see if there is a colleague willing to try it on the same day as you, then compare notes. Churchill said that failure is not fatal and success is not final; those engaged in a group effort can surface the mistakes, agree on how to fix them, and move ahead with the improvements in place. My two most successful and satisfying years in the classroom came as the social studies teacher on the seventh-grade inclusion team. The synergy that comes from working with others who share the same goals (and the same commitment to improvement) is a tangible thing; I made great strides at becoming a better teacher with the help of colleagues willing to take risks on a daily basis.

The best teachers whom I have met and observed over the course of the last three decades are too busy looking after the best interests of students to spend time complaining about things outside their control. In the face of problems, they seek solutions. The finest principal I ever knew insisted that her teachers and staff do what is best for children, and everything flowed from that. Naysayers and negaholics need not apply.

CHAPTER 48
THE EXTRA MILE

I grew up in a small town of maybe 5,000 residents. We had one elementary school and a junior-senior high school. In those pre-mall, pre-Walmart days, we had a relatively small downtown with plenty of shopping opportunities. We boasted our own hometown newspaper, *The North East Breeze*, and a beautiful community library where I spent countless hours on a stool, reading mystery stories and biographies of famous people. What we did not have in our little town was a recreation center, somewhere to go for kids after school or on weekends, and someplace for adults to gather for various activities.

Several of us in our eighth-grade class (this was 1962) decided it would be great to have a YMCA in town, and we found a willing project partner in our eighth-grade reading teacher, Mrs. Krause. Nothing in her contract, I'm pretty sure, said anything about helping a bunch of rambunctious and ambitious teenagers undertake what turned out to be a significant—and ultimately successful—endeavor. She suggested we canvass the adults in town to find out if they would support a YMCA, and she helped us with the document. Also, she suggested some contacts among the merchants in town, as to a possible location. There being no municipal funds for a new building, something up on the second floor of one of the businesses downtown would have to do. And it did. As freshmen, we worked with students from the Catholic school in town to clean and refurbish a good deal of second-floor footage above several existing businesses. The YMCA was a success.

But it would not have gotten off the ground had it not been for Mrs. Krause. She believed in us, and she became involved in ways that helped us turn our dream into reality. I have never forgotten her assistance and

CHAPTER 48

encouragement early on in the project, and it reminds me once again that teachers who go the extra mile are appreciated long after the dust settles on a particular school year. It is a reminder that we teach students, not content. The teacher who puts in untold extra hours as a junior-class adviser, or the teacher who goes to the principal to ask if he can start a chess club after hours will both be remembered as extra-mile adults who are willing to give their own time, often for very little—or no—extra monetary compensation. To such professionals, the result is compensation enough.

I have written elsewhere (Nash, 2011) about an elementary cafeteria manager who chose to work one of two registers at the point of sale in his cafeteria. He wore a funny hat (a hot dog, when I met him) every day, *and he greeted every student by name as they approached the register.* Let me say that again: He greeted every student by name. According to his principal, Kathy Hwang, the students loved him. He realized his job was less about food and more about kids, and his willingness to go the extra mile led to his promotion shortly after I met him in 2009. It takes time, effort, and commitment to learn the names of students and interact with them every day, but it is a prime example of a willingness to go the extra mile for kids.

Recently I did a walk-through with Gene Soltner, then the principal of Great Neck Middle School (VA), just before school started the first day after spring break. We traveled through every hallway in a three-story building, and he greeted every student and teacher we saw, using the names of the students and asking about one thing or another they were involved in. Soltner also involves his PLC lead teachers in the hiring process, something other principals may be unwilling to do. Everything I saw during my lengthy morning visit told me that this is a principal willing on a regular basis to go the extra mile.

In my last teaching post, twenty years after my first job, I made it a point, as did all the teachers on my middle school team, to call parents in the week before students reported. This carried over into the first week of school for our students, and I was pleased—and amazed, frankly—at the reception we got. Seems no one had done that before. The kids whose parents had not been called wanted to make sure we called home. Remember, these phone calls were meant to begin the process of developing relationships that would serve us, those parents, and their students all year long. Here is the topper: "Those" phone calls, the ones we often don't want to make, later in the school year went better because we had shown a willingness to develop those relationships early. This was the idea of the special education teacher on our inclusion team, and it was a good one. And it proved to us that going the extra mile is worth it.

The most important perspective when it comes to this behavior on the part of teachers is that of the students. Your average sophomore has been around the educational block a few times in his career as a student, and she knows which teachers are putting in their time—and possibly wasting the time of the student—and which ones gladly put in the extra effort. Kids know who is sincere and who is disingenuous. They see teachers run out the door every day just behind—or just before—the buses leave. They know which teachers are there early, and which teachers are there for them on a consistent basis.

Students prefer teachers willing to go that extra mile on their behalf.

Build a Better Classroom by Going the Extra Mile

As soon as your rosters are available in the week before students report, consider beginning the process of calling home to introduce yourself. I know schools have evenings devoted to open houses, but the phone calls are personal, they reach almost everyone, and they are not limited to ten minutes before the bell rings and all the parents run out the door to their son's or daughter's next class. At open house, parents meet many teachers and have few substantive conversations. Most open houses in which I have participated over the years are rushed events, not contemplative ones that allow you to really get to know parents and guardians.

Extra-curricular activities abound in school districts, and they provide students with great opportunities to display and hone their various talents. After

CHAPTER 48

attending a concert band performance, several students thanked me for attending. I didn't realize they knew I had been there, but students know where their support lies with faculty members. That concert was the first indication to me that I had several students who were active—and incredibly talented—members of the school's music program. My suggestion to new teachers is that one of the best ways to begin to build relationships with students is to find ways to go the extra mile for them.

CHAPTER 49
THE POWER OF COLLABORATION

As I listened in on a team meeting several years ago, one of the teachers excitedly shared a bit of research she had discovered the night before. A discussion followed, including ways to incorporate the research into the best practices of the team. On social media outlets, scores of discoveries on the part of teachers at every grade level and subject area pop up every week. Requests from teachers for information, ideas, or classroom experiences related to this or that topic are answered quickly. Kids are apparently not the only ones with inquiring minds, and social media, along with increasingly frequent grade-level meetings around the country, all make sharing a valuable part of the improvement process.

Teaching can be a lonely exercise if teachers choose to keep the door closed and do this year what they did last year, with few improvements. I was guilty of that, as were many of my colleagues, in my early years as a classroom teacher at the junior high and high school levels. In my travels around the country, I notice that in most schools, especially at the secondary level, teachers work in isolation. Barth (1991) says we have come to like it this way: "God didn't create self-contained classrooms, fifty-minute periods,

THE BIGGEST ROOM IN THE WORLD IS THE ROOM FOR IMPROVEMENT.

CHAPTER 49

and subjects taught in isolation. We did, because we find working alone safer and more preferable to working together" (p. 128). As I have often said, the status quo is a powerful taskmaster.

One of the problems with putting teachers together in reflective groups is that members of the group may see the exercise as an evaluative process, one where colleagues may be in a position to judge, rather than help each other in a more formative structure. When teachers open their doors to colleagues as part of a collaborative reflective process, it should not be evaluative, affirm Hord and Sommers (2008). It should be a process centered around "peers helping peers that includes teachers visiting each other's classrooms on a regular basis to observe, take notes, and discuss their observations with the teacher they have visited. In this way, teachers facilitate the work of changing practice with each other" (p. 15). Again, the goal is to support, not judge. This needs to be clear upfront, and the feedback provided by observing teachers should not be judgmental in any way. Feedback is just feedback, and feedback is the lifeblood of continuous improvement.

Peer observation, says Brookfield (1995), "must be reciprocal. If you are going to invite colleagues into your classrooms, it should be on the understanding that you'll return the favor by visiting theirs" (p. 85). When asked by teachers what a visitor should look for, I suggest the teacher being visited (the word observed has an evaluative connotation) ask the visitor to look for one or two things only. For example, the teacher could ask the visitor to look for how she handles wait time (after she asks a question or after she receives an answer; wait time is important in each instance). Another question might involve the clarity of directions. The point here is that an observer with a "balcony view" can see and process things a busy, engaged teacher can't. Take care to reciprocate, setting up a date and time for you to visit your colleague's classroom. Ask what it is he or she would like you to look for while you are there.

I have visited schools where time is built in for grade-level collaboration. Learning targets and the steps to meet them can make for a substantive conversation; eventually, the proof is in the evidence. *Is there evidence that what we did collectively in our classrooms succeeded in helping all students meet or exceed the goals set upfront?* My experience is that working together is more interesting, fun, and rewarding than working in isolation. My two best years in the classroom came as part of a seventh-grade inclusion team. DuFour (2015), citing Hattie (2009), draws a stark contrast between attempts at personal reflection and collaborative reflection: "There is no evidence that reflective preparation and teaching by an isolated teacher have a positive impact on student learning; however, there is abundant evidence that reflective teaching is powerful when it is collective and based on evidence of student learning." Then comes the lament: "Yet there are educators who insist they must have five hours of personal planning time each week while they resist devoting even one hour to collaborative work" (p. 131). I have seen this over and over again, and I and my teaching colleagues would have fought giving up prep time.

This is where leadership comes in. It is the job of building administrators to find the time for reflective collaboration, and then to make sure that time is used wisely. As teachers work together toward specific instructional targets, leadership teams should be part of that effort. I was recently in an elementary school where each of the grade-level teams met with leadership during the course of a teacher workday. Hord and Sommers (2008) point out that

> It is not enough to say we believe in staff learning, we have to demonstrate that by meeting, learning together, sharing knowledge and skills. Again, collegial learning—not just the words—creates professional learning communities. When the principal sustains focus on staff learning, student learning increases. Teachers who function at higher cognitive levels produce students who function at higher cognitive levels. (p. 29)

When school improvement plans are created from the bottom up, rather than handed down from the top, teachers are invested in the processes and the outcomes. Teams of teachers working together with a clear idea of where they want to go—and how they will get there—are in a much better position to make steady progress than individual teachers working on their own. Rick DuFour (2015) issues a challenge to all of us: "Until teachers and administrators acknowledge their responsibility for perpetuating isolation and commit to creating a new culture of schooling, little is likely to change" (p. 124). I have seen first-hand what can be done when teachers and administrators make the decision to change.

CHAPTER 49

Build Better Classrooms with Collaborative Reflection

In the course of more than five decades in education, I have seen massive—and expensive—improvement programs come and go. So much time is spent planning and preparing for the program's debut that everyone out in the schools gets nervous. They hear rumors and listen to the negaholics in the faculty lounges, and the pushback begins. Trying to get something off the ground and into the air at the district level is, in the best of circumstances, a gargantuan task. But leadership teams and teams of teachers can accomplish a great deal on behalf of kids.

The key is to make the commitment to a true professional learning community, with teachers and administrators committed to helping classroom teachers get better at getting better, with the result that gaps are closed and students are prepared for their futures, not for our past. I'm not a big proponent of teacher evaluation systems; at a recent conference I heard Dylan Wiliam say he was too busy helping teachers improve to worry overmuch about formal evaluations of teachers. Every teacher is at a different level in his or her development and effectiveness, and every teacher can improve. The best way to do that is in the company of colleagues who work together every day to help students meet learning goals, develop intellectually, and learn the myriad practical skills they will need when they graduate.

CHAPTER 50
LOOKING BACK AT THOSE WHO LOOK FORWARD

I've had the good fortune over the past eighteen years to meet, listen to, work with, and learn from people who have dedicated their lives to looking forward. One of them, Kathy Hwang, is no longer with us, but she touched the lives of thousands of children as a teacher and principal. In the latter role, she insisted that her staff (all of them, from classrooms to the cafeteria) ask themselves one question every day: "Is what I'm doing best for children?" Every day she had students read to her in her office. Every day her goal was to visit at least three classrooms, and continuous improvement was her mantra. Getting better at getting better was a collective effort at Sanders Corner Elementary (VA). She believed that everyone in the building "must know that steady forward progress, in every sense of the word, is a given—and is not negotiable" (Nash and Hwang, 2013, p. 12). She believed that the pressure to improve, in the words of Laurel Schmidt (2002), should be gently but relentlessly applied.

One of Kathy's favorite books was the book I just cited, Schmidt's *Gardening in the Minefield: A Survival Guide for Administrators* (2002). Chapter 7 in the book is entitled "Do Nothing for Staff That They Can Do for Themselves." Schmidt offers this advice to building administrators: "Stop wasting time in fruitless meetings. Reorganize the work of the school into projects, so that staff members address all issues that don't require your personal stewardship" (p. 72). Schmidt's honesty and sense of humor pervade her book, no more so than when she laments the fact that we don't harness the power, experience, and knowledge of our teachers in the continuous improvement process.

CHAPTER 50

> One of the great paradoxes of education is that we entrust teachers with our most precious resource, then turn around and treat them like parolees or overgrown children. We abandon them to teach unevaluated for years but won't let them into the supply closet without an escort. If we're long on kids and short on texts, we post an armed guard at the book room. (p. 70)

Kathy Hwang understood that the resources needed to set and meet learning goals were already in the building, and she made sure that teachers and other staff members were part of the continuous improvement process. The SIP (School Improvement Plan) was created by, implemented by, evaluated by, and improved by her teacher teams.

In March of 2019, I had the good fortune of walking through the doors of Lovejoy Elementary School in Des Moines, Iowa, where the hallways are filled with artwork done by the students, and where, on that afternoon, a conference room was filled with the members of a grade-level team, the principal, dean of students, and three instructional coaches, all working on plans of action for the way forward for the third-grade students. The leadership team at Lovejoy meets at 6:00 a.m. every Wednesday morning, where they discuss their own plan of action for the coming week and ask some pertinent questions: *What are we seeing and hearing?* and *How can we better support our teachers?* The plan for coaching in classrooms is also visited during that early morning hour. Like Kathy Hwang, Shelly Pospeshil, Lovejoy's principal, has a system of improvement in place that operates on its own in the best interests of children.

Schools like Sanders Corner and Lovejoy offer proof that professional learning communities work, and, as Laurel Schmidt believes, that principals should never do for teachers and staff what they can do for themselves and the students they serve. The resources, the energy, the expertise, and the experience are there in the building, waiting to be tapped.

By contrast, I have been in schools where doors—and minds—are often closed, where working in teams "was tried a few years ago, but didn't take." I've been in faculty lounges where the chief topic of conversation is who has the fewest years left until retirement. One teacher told me she appreciated what I had shared with her, but she had been doing what she was doing in her classroom for twenty-five years, and wasn't about to change. Actually, the students I observed in her classroom could

LOOKING BACK AT THOSE WHO ALWAYS LOOK FORWARD

have told me the same thing; they had been doing what they had been doing in that classroom for the last several months, and it wasn't about to change. Teachers who constantly think about retirement are, I have found, in classrooms with students who constantly think about the bell that will set them free—if temporarily.

I think often about those administrators and teachers who are always looking forward. They are dedicated to getting better at getting better, and their students are fortunate indeed to be in those schools and classrooms. It is a pleasure to walk through a building where negativity is nowhere to be found, and where students, teachers, administrators, office staff, custodians, and cafeteria employees want to be there every day.

And I think of the cafeteria manager in the funny hat at the cash register every day, greeting students by name and letting them know they were in a special place. I think of teachers who are not afraid to take risks on behalf of the children they serve, and I think of administrators who harness the power of the human capital in the building; successful and forward-looking principals know that all the resources they need to succeed are right there in the building. I think of the custodian who sat down next to a primary student and asked her to read to him. The best things we do are often not in the contracts we sign. The best things we do get done because we know it is right for kids.

Great teachers, I have found, have vision, and they share that vision with their students. They see things as they *can* be, and they take the necessary risks to get there. And great administrators encourage the taking of risks, if they are taken on behalf of students.

AFTERWORD

When I am presenting to teachers, I often conclude by asking them to identify one of their favorite teachers, then explain to their shoulder partner why those teachers were so important to them. I don't have to hear what those workshop participants are saying to know how much those teachers meant to them; I watch their body language and listen to the laughter. I see the occasional tears that underline the emotional impact those teachers had on them, perhaps decades ago. As I walk around the room, I hear snatches of stories they may or may not be sharing for the first time.

And when I ask if those favorite teachers took the time to build a relationship with them, all the hands go up. And then I often share, if I am with a group of secondary teachers, a story about my favorite high school teacher, Frances Roggenbaum. She taught English, and I learned style and grammar at her feet when it came to writing. Our senior year was devoted to British Literature, and one memorable afternoon, I was tasked with reading one stanza of Coleridge's epic poem, *The Rime of the Ancient Mariner*, in preparation for explaining and interpreting those lines to my classmates. Alas, I wasn't doing as instructed on that occasion; I was absorbed in one of William Somerset Maugham's short stories, one which I had discovered in the textbook, many pages removed from poetry which interested me far less than prose.

Mrs. Roggenbaum moved about the room, asking guided questions of my classmates as they worked on one stanza or another of the poem, then came up beside me. She took in the scene, gave me the look, and walked away. I quickly shifted my attention from Maugham back to Coleridge, and thought little of it. She never brought up my indiscretion, and I did what I remember to be a creditable job of interpreting my stanza of Coleridge's poem in front of my classmates.

For Christmas that year, my Aunt Millie gave me a two-volume set entitled *The Complete Works of W. Somerset Maugham*. I looked at her, grateful, of course, but curious. I had never said anything about that author to her. When I asked how she knew I enjoyed Maugham's work, she smiled and said that a "little bird" had told her. The feathered friend in question turned out to be Mrs. Roggenbaum, who had called my aunt and told her that the Book of the Month Club had this two-volume set for sale for the holidays.

I have known compliance and control teachers—and I was one—who would have lowered the proverbial boom on me that afternoon when my in-class transgression became apparent. But Mrs. Roggenbaum didn't lower any booms; she picked up the phone. And when I graduated, she took me aside and encouraged me to not be content with a B.S. in Education, but to take the additional two years to complete a post-graduate degree. I made it a point to go to her third-floor classroom one day several years later, show her my Master of Arts in History degree, and thank her for all that she had done for me in the three years I spent in her classroom.

No amount of tax money spent on curriculum, pacing guides, textbooks, computers, furniture, HVAC systems, or interactive screens can result in the kind of *impact* a teacher with a personal commitment to create a safe, wondrous, engaging, and exciting environment can deliver. And no amount of hardware or software can make up for a teacher who ignores the big little things I have laid out in this book. The teacher who demands respect, then yells at students, is guilty of the kind of incongruent behavior that, by definition, is at odds with what she is demanding from her students. I observed this very unfortunate behavior on the part of a teacher years ago, and it was not pretty. The curriculum might have been sound, and the computer software might have been superb, but it makes no difference if teachers do not attend to the big little things that create an effective and enjoyable learning environment.

I firmly believe that all of the truly exceptional teachers I have observed and coached over the years—at all levels—*have taken the time to build excellent relationships with their students*, and they have created safe and comfortable classroom environments where students can also

AFTERWORD

develop solid working relationships with their peers. Jacobs and Zmuda, in *Streamlining the Curriculum* (2023), write the following:

> Imagine walking into a learning space and being immediately struck by the productive hum, rhythm, and vitality of the participants in the room. Learners clustered around a table intensely debate an idea and how to improve on it. In another space, chill music emanates from portable speakers. Across the hall, learners are sitting in low cushioned chairs or sprawled on the floor, immersed in their individual reading or viewing experiences. (p. 25)

I have been in those classes on countless occasions. I walked into a high school science classroom where students were standing, moving, and collaborating in a way that told me that what I was seeing was business as usual for them. I was met at the door by a student who showed me his portfolio, then introduced me to the teacher, who told me she really started teaching when she realized she was not the only teacher in the room. Agency and collaboration walked hand in hand in there. And her students told me they loved coming to that classroom every other day. They also admitted that they were clock-watchers in other classrooms in that same building. Positive working relationships made the "productive hum and rhythm" of those learners possible.

In *Every Connection Matters* (2024), Michael and Nita Creekmore assert that "Teacher-to-student relationships are important because without a solid, positive relationship, learning cannot happen." I agree with those authors when they go on to say that "the relationships that we form with students are what keeps us coming back year after year" (p. 35). When I have post-observation discussions with teachers who obviously love teaching, I know—because I have just seen it first-hand—that the relationships they have forged with their students play a big part in keeping them coming back for more.

REFERENCES

Abeles, V.
    (2015). *Beyond measure: Rescuing an overscheduled, overtested, underestimated generation.* New York: Simon & Schuster.

Aguilar, E.
    (2018). *Onward: Cultivating emotional resilience in educators.* San Francisco, CA: Jossey-Bass.

Allen, R.
    (2008). *Green light classrooms: Teaching techniques that accelerate learning.* Thousand Oaks, CA: Corwin.

Allen, R. H.
    (2014). *High-impact teaching strategies for the xyz era of education.* Boston, MA: Pearson.

Allen, R., & Hann, M.
    (2012). *Humane presentations: A commitment to the alleviation of suffering.* Morabbin, Victoria: Hawker Brownlow Education.

Allen, R. H.
    (2002). *Impact teaching: Ideas and strategies for teachers to maximize student learning.* Boston, MA: Allyn & Bacon.

Allen, R., & Scozzi, N.
    (2012). *Sparking student synapses, 9–12: Think critically and accelerate learning.* Thousand Oaks, CA: Corwin.

Allen, R., & Wood, W.W,
    (2013). *The rock 'n' roll classroom: Using music to manage mood, energy, and learning.* Thousand Oaks, CA: Corwin.

Almarode, J., & Miller, A.
    (2013). *From snorkelers to scuba divers in the elementary science classroom: Strategies and lessons that move students toward deeper learning.* Thousand Oaks, CA: Corwin.

REFERENCES

Anderson, M.
>(2019). *What we say and how we say it matter: Teacher talk that improves student learning and behavior.* Alexandria, VA: ASCD.

Bailey, B.
>(2001). *Conscious discipline: 7 basic skills for brain smart classroom management.* Oviedo, FL: Loving Guidance.

Barth, R. S.
>(1991). Restructuring schools: Some questions for teachers and principals. *Phi Delta Kappan, 73*(2), 123–128.

Bender, W. N.
>(2012). *Project-based learning: Differentiating instruction for the 21st century.* Thousand Oaks, CA: Corwin.

Bluestein, J.
>(2010). *Becoming a win-win teacher: Survival strategies for the beginning educator.* New York: Skyhorse.

Bluestein, J.
>(2001). *Creating emotionally safe schools: A guide for educators and parents.* Deerfield Beach, FL: Health Communications.

Boss, S., & Larmer, J.
>(2018). *Project based teaching: How to create rigorous and engaging learning experiences.* Alexandria, VA: ASCD.

Brookfield, S. D.
>(1995). *Becoming a critically effective teacher.* San Francisco, CA: Jossey-Bass.

Brookhart, S. M.
>(2024). *Classroom assessment essentials.* Alexandria, VA: ASCD.

Caine, R. N., & Caine, G.
>(1994). *Making connections: Teaching and the human brain.* Menlo Park, CA: Addison-Wesley.

Costa, A.
>(2008). *The school as a home for the mind: Creating mindful curriculum, instruction, and dialogue.* Thousand Oaks, CA: Corwin Press.

Creekmore, M., & Creekmore, N.
>(2024). *Every connection matters: How to build, maintain, and restore relationships inside the classroom and out.* Alexandria, VA: ASCD.

Curwin, R. L., Mendler, A. N., & Mendler, B. D.
>(2018). *Discipline with dignity: How to build responsibility, relationships, and respect in your classroom.* Alexandria, VA: ASCD.

Denton, P.
>(2015). *The power of our words: Teacher language that helps children learn* (2nd ed.). Turners Falls, MA: Center for Responsive Schools, Inc.

REFERENCES

DuFour, R.
(2015). *In praise of American educators: And how they can become even better.* Bloomington, IN: Solution Tree.

Farson, R., & Keyes, R.
(2002). *Whoever makes the most mistakes wins: The paradox of innovation.* New York: The Free Press.

Fisher, D., Frey, N., & Law, N.
(2021). *Comprehension: The skill, will, and thrill of reading.* Thousand Oaks, CA: Corwin.

Fogarty, R. J., Kerns, G. M., & Pete, B. M.
(2018). *Unlocking student talent: The new science of developing expertise.* New York: Teachers College Press.

France, P. E.
(2023). *Make teaching sustainable: Six shifts that teachers want and students need.* Alexandria, VA: ASCD.

Frey, N., Fisher, D., & Smith, D.
(2019). *All learning is social and emotional: Helping students develop essential skills for the classroom and beyond.* Alexandria, VA: ASCD.

Fried, R. L.
(2001). *The passionate teacher.* (2nd ed.). Boston, MA: Beacon Press.

Fullan, M.
(2010). *Motion leadership: The skinny on becoming change savvy.* Thousand Oaks, CA: Corwin.

Garmston, R. J.
(2019). *The astonishing power of storytelling: Leading, teaching, and transforming in a new way.* Thousand Oaks, CA: Corwin.

Garmston, R. J.
(2018). *The presenter's fieldbook: A practical guide.* Lanham, MD: Rowman & Littlefield.

Garmston, R., & Wellman, B.
(1992). *How to make presentations that teach and transform.* Alexandria, VA: ASCD.

Garrison, D. R.
(2016). *Thinking collaboratively: Learning in a community of inquiry.* New York: Routledge.

Gershon, M.
(2018). *How to manage behavior in the classroom: The complete guide.* West Palm Beach, FL: Learning Sciences International.

REFERENCES

Gunter, M. A., Estes. T. H., & Schwab, J.
  (2003). *Instruction: A models approach* (4th ed.). Boston, MA: Pearson Education.

Hall, P., & Simeral, A.
  (2015). *Teach, reflect, learn: Building your capacity for success in the classroom.* Alexandria, VA: ASCD.

Hallowell, E. M., & Ratey, J. J.
  (2022). *ADHD 2.0: New science and essential strategies for thriving with distraction—from childhood through adulthood.* New York: Ballantine Books.

Hattie, J.
  (2009). *Visible learning: A synthesis of over 800 meta-analyses relating to achievement.* New York: Routledge.

Hattie, J.
  (2023). *Visible learning: The sequel: A synthesis of over 2,100 meta analyses relating to achievement.* New York: Routledge.

Hattie, J., & Clarke, S.
  (2019). *Visible learning feedback.* New York: Routledge.

Hattie, J., & Zierer, K.
  (2018). *10 mindframes for visible learning: Teaching for success.* New York: Routledge.

Hoff, R.
  (1992). *I can see you naked.* Kansas City, MO: Andrews and McMeel.

Hord, S. M., & Sommers, W. A.
  (2008). *Leading professional learning communities.* Thousand Oaks, CA: Corwin.

Jacobs, H. H., & Zmuda, A.
  (2023). *Streamlining the curriculum: Using the storyboard approach to frame compelling learning journeys.* Alexandria, VA: ASCD.

Jenkins, L.
  (2003). *Improving student learning: Applying Deming's quality principles in the classroom* (2nd ed.). Milwaukee, WI: ASQ.

Jones, F.
  (2007). *Tools for teaching: Discipline, instruction, motivation.* Santa Cruz, CA: Fredric H. Jones & Associates, Inc.

Kagan, S.
  (1994). *Cooperative learning.* San Clemente, CA: Kagan Cooperative Learning.

Kohn, A.
  (2006). *Beyond discipline: From compliance to community.* Alexandria, VA: ASCD.

REFERENCES

McTighe, J., & Willis, J.
    (2019). *Upgrade your teaching: Understanding by design meets neuroscience.* Alexandria, VA: ASCD.

Medina, J.
    (2014). *Brain rules: 12 principles for surviving and thriving at work, home, and school* (2nd ed.). Seattle, WA: Pear Press.

Nash, R.
    (2011). *Harness the power of reflection: Continuous school improvement from the front office to the classroom.* Thousand Oaks, CA: Corwin.

Nash, R.
    (2019). *In praise of foibles: The impact of mistakes, failure, and fear on continuous improvement in schools.* West Palm Beach, FL: Learning Sciences International.

Nash, R. (2014). *The active classroom: Practical strategies for involving students in the learning process*
    (2nd ed.). Thousand Oaks, CA: Corwin.

Nash, R.
    (2010). *The active classroom field book: Success stories from the active classroom.* Thousand Oaks, CA: Corwin.

Nash, R., & Hwang, K.
    (2013). *Collaborative school leadership: Practical strategies for principals.* Lanham, MD: Rowman & Littlefield.

Orr, J.
    (2022). *Demystifying discussion: How to teach and assess academic conversation skills, K-5.* Alexandria, VA: ASCD.

Posey, A.
    (2019). *Engage the brain: How to design learning that taps into the power of emotion.* Alexandria, VA: ASCD.

Ratey, J.
    (2008). *Spark: The revolutionary new science of exercise and the brain.* New York: Little, Brown and Company.

Rowe, M.
    (1986). Wait time: Slowing down may be a way of speeding up! *Journal of Teacher Education, 37*(1), 43–50.

Schmidt, L.
    (2002). *Gardening in the minefield: A survival guide for school administrators.* Portsmouth, NH: Heinemann.

Serravallo, J.
    (2021). *Teaching writing in small groups.* Portsmouth, NH: Heinemann.

REFERENCES

Silver, D., & Berckenmeyer, J. C.
(2023). *Deliberate optimism: Still reclaiming the joy in education* (2nd ed.). Thousand Oaks, CA: Corwin.

Stiggins, R. J., & Chappuis, J.
(2012). *An introduction to student-involved assessment for learning* (6th ed.). Boston, MA: Pearson.

Syed, M.
(2015). *Black box thinking: Why most people never learn from their mistakes—but some do.* New York: Portfolio/Penguin.

Tate, M. L.
(2012). *'Sit and get' won't grow dendrites: 20 professional learning strategies that engage the adult brain.* Thousand Oaks, CA: Corwin.

Twenge, J. M.
(2017). *iGen: Why today's super-connected kids are growing up less rebellious, more tolerant, less happy—and completely unprepared for adulthood, and what that means for the rest of us.* New York: Atria.

Wagner, T.
(2014). *The global achievement gap: Why even our best schools don't teach the new survival skills our children need—and what we can do about it* (revised and updated edition). New York: Basic Books.

Wagner, T., & Dintersmith, T.
(2015). *Most likely to succeed: Preparing our kids for the innovation era.* New York: Scribner.

Walsh, J. A., & Sattes, B D.
(2015). *Questioning for classroom discussion: Purposeful speaking, engaged listening, deep thinking.* Alexandria, VA: ASCD.

White, K.
(2017). *Softening the edges: Assessment practices that honor K-12 teachers and learners.* Bloomington, IN: Solution Tree.

White, K.
(2022). *Student self assessment: Data notebooks, portfolios, & other tools to advance learning.* Bloomington, IL: Solution Tree.

White, K.
(2019). *UNLOCKED: Assessment as the key to everyday creativity in the classroom.* Bloomington, IN: Solution Tree.

Wilson, D., & Conyers, M.
(2020). *Developing growth mindsets: Maximizing students' potential.* Alexandria, VA: ASCD.

Wilson, M. B.
(2016). *Interactive modeling: A powerful technique for teaching children*. Turners Falls, MA: Center for Responsive Schools.

Wyatt, R. L., & White, J. E.
(2007). *Making your first year a success* (2nd ed.). Thousand Oaks, CA: Corwin.

Zoller, K., & Landry, C.
(2010). *The choreography of presenting: The 7 essential abilities of effective presenters*. Thousand Oaks, CA: Corwin.

Zwiers, J.
(2020). *The communication effect: How to enhance learning by building ideas and bridging information gaps*. Thousand Oaks, CA: Corwin.

Zwiers, J.
(2019). *Next steps with academic conversations: New ideas for improving learning through classroom talk*. Portsmouth, NH: Stenhouse.

Zwiers, J., & Crawford, M.
(2011). *Academic conversations: Classroom talk that fosters critical thinking and content understandings*. Portland, ME: Stenhouse.

INDEX

Note: Page numbers in "*Italics*" represents figures in the text.

Abeles, V., 35
abolitionism, 169
access to complex tasks, 107–10
active listening, 161
ADHD 2.0, 185–86
adult-centered classroom, 32, 33
Aguilar, E., 193
Allen, R.H., 19, 28, 56, 73, 141, 142, 183, 185, 187
Almarode, J., 33
Anderson, M., 23, 24, 39, 40
appointment-clock partners, 63
arms control, 137–40
Art Costa, 162
assessment-related questions, 175–76
The Astonishing Power of Storytelling (Garmston), 112
auditory, 96, 120, 129–32, 134, 137, 149, 151, 156

Baenen, 192
Bailey, B., 191, 192
Barth, R.S., 203
Bell, Brittan, 12
Bender, W.N., 103, 104
Berckenmeyer, J.C., 192, 195
Big Little Things, 4, 5
blame game avoidance, 191–94
Bluestein, J., 38, 44, 165

body language, 19, 130, 138–40, 163, 167, 168, 180, 211; of speakers and listeners, 50; of students, 1, 2, 8, 19, 153, 158, 161
boredom, 158, 195
Bose SoundDock, 27, 141
Boss, S., 12, 105
brainstorming procedures, 12, 13, 70, 95, 103–5
Brittan Bell's third-grade classroom, *11*, 12
Brookfield, S.D., 204
Brookhart, Susan, 174
built-in state changes, 187–90

Caine, G., 169
Caine, R.N., 169
calming effect, 44
can-do outlook, 193–94
Chappuis, J., 88
The Chicken Dance, 184
choice, 11–14
Churchill, Winston, 19, 197
clarify/support questions, 177, 178
clarity, 13, 19, 49, 65, 72, 99, 100, 177, 204
Clarke, S., 87, 92, 179
Classroom Assessment Essentials (Brookhart), 174
collaborative classroom environment, 7

INDEX

collaborative learning, 59, 189
collaborative reflection, *203*, 203–6
comfort zones, moving students outside, 9–10
command voice, 48, 96, 97
communication skills, 5, 10
The Complete Works of W. Somerset Maugham, 212
compliance-and-control environments, 3, 11
Comprehension: The Skill, Will, and Thrill of Reading (Fisher, Frey, and Law), 170
confidence, 76, 78, 100
congruence, 19–21
consistency, 16
content-related query, 71
conversational voices, 96
Costa, A., 48, 162, 163
Crawford, M., 63, 78
Creekmore, N., 213
critical-thinking skills, 78
Cupp, Darcy, 16
Curwin, R.L., 25

deep-level learners, 33
Demystifying Discussion (Jennifer), 161
Denton, P., 166
depression, 187
Developing Growth Mindsets (Wilson and Conyers), 184
Dintersmith, T., 25
dipstick checks, 83–86
directions in classrooms, 19
do-as-I-do principle, 21
dopamine, 38, 142, 185
DuFour, R., 205

effectively working the room, 145–48
effective visual support, 125–27
emotional safety, 38, 167
emotions, 35, 44, 169, 171
empathy, 26, 47–48, 103, 163, 171
encouraging using good questions, *178*, 180–81

Estes. T.H., 78
Every Connection Matters (Michael and Creekmore), 213
extra-curricular activities, 201
extra mile, 199–202, *201*

face-to-face conversations, 63
failure, 28, 32, 34, 81, 83, 93, 173, 192, 193, 196, 197
Farson, R., 24
favorite teachers, 211
fear factor, 23–26, *26*
fear of making a mistake, 23
feedback, 7–10, 21, 24, 32, 33, 81–90, 92, 93, 105–7, 109, 116, 121, 122, 135, 148, 158, 167, 173, 174, 176, 179, 189, 190, 204
fight-flight reflex, 43
Fisher, D., 32, 92, 146, 170, 189
flexible seating, *11*, 12, 59, 60
Fogarty, R.J., 8
font, 125–26
formative assessment, 105
framing, 28
France, P.E., 2
Frey, N., 32, 92, 146, 170, 189
Friday's quiz/test, 36
Fried, R.L., 32, 166
frustration, 3, 8, 15, 28, 67, 81, 95, 150, 152
Fullan, Michael, 80–82

Galford, Kathy, 68, 69
Gardening in the Minefield: A Survival Guide for Administrators (Schmidt), 207
Garmston, Bob, 112, 113, 133, 134, 138
Garmston, Robert, 135, 171
Garrison, D.R., 51
gear-shifting moments, 96
genuine praise, 92
Gershon, M., 44, 91, 92
good questions, 177–81
grade-level collaboration, 204

INDEX

guiding questions, 146
Gunter, M.A., 78

Haines, Joel, 36, 169, 172
Hall, P., 196
Hallowell, E.M., 185
hand gestures, 19, 137, 138
Hann, M., 28
Hattie, J., 87, 92, 158, 174, 179, 180, 205
have-at-it spirit, 79–82
Hoff, Ron, 111, 133
Hord, S.M., 204, 205
humiliation, 25, 38
humor, 36–38, 147, 167, 207
Hwang, Kathy, 200, 207, 208

inactivity in classrooms, 195
incongruence, 20
innovation, 3, 25, 170, 197
instructional innovation, 3
interactive classrooms, 10, 97, 107, 108, 126, 146, 150
Interactive Modeling (Wilson), 150
interpersonal skills, 158

Jacobs, H.H., 213
Jenkins, Lee, 194
Jones, Fred, 43

Kagan, S., 55, 72
Kenison, Chuck, 167
Kennedy, John F., 19
Kerns, G.M., 8
Keyes, R., 24
King, Martin Luther, Jr., 19
Kohn, A., 45
Konrad, Emily, 59, 60

Landry, C., 167
Larmer, J., 12, 105
last impressions, 115–17
laughter, 36–38, 111, 112, 115, 116, 211
learners-in-chief, 1
learning names, 39–41

learning pool, 31–34
learning targets, 9
lesson plans, 15, 79
listening skills, 5, 13, 47–53, 65, 71–73, 76, 77, 80, 103–6, 109, 115, 116, 119, 133, 134, 138, 148, 161, 163, 164, 178–80
Lombardi, Vince, 16

Marshall, Mary, 64
Maugham, William Somerset, 211
McTighe, J., 61
Medina, John, 69, 129, 142
Mendler, A.N., 25
Mendler, B.D., 25
mental states of participants, 35–38
Michael, 213
Miller, A., 33
Motion Leadership (Fullan), 82
movement, 59–62, *61*
multiple pairing techniques, 67–70
Murphy's law, 3, 67
music, 24, 35–37, 57, 60, 69, 70, 98, 112, 115, *141*, 141–43, 162, 165, 188, 202, 213

Nag, Nag, Nag, 43
negaholics, 193, 196, 197, 206
Newburn, Rebecca, 105
nonthreatening environment, 81
Norfar, Telannia, 12, 13
novelty, 183–86
nuts-and-bolts instructional processes, 99

one-at-a-time directions, 153–56
on-the-job training, 79
open-ended questions, 77
opening bell, 111–13
open palm gesture, 137
oral language skills, 10, 14, 78, 106, 107, 139
Orbison, Roy, 115
Orr, J., 161
own learning, 158–60

INDEX

paired conversations, 73
pair share, 56
paraphrasing, 161–64
The Passionate Teacher (Fried), 166
patience, 9, 53, 77
PBL tasks and projects, 106
peer observation, 204
perfect practice, 15–16
permanent learning partners, 57, 63–65
Pete, B.M., 8
physical and mental state of students, 188–89
physical gestures, 134
physical states of participants, 35–38
planning and practice, 119–23
Posey, A., 7, 35
positive gestures, 138–40
positive thinking, 196, *196*
Pospeshil, Shelly, 208
PowerPoint, 4, 27, 103, 119, 122, 125, 132
presentation programs, 27, 103, 119, 125, 126
presentation skills, 103, 123, 135, 138
The Presenter's Fieldbook (Garmston), 134
press and release, 55–58, *57*, 154
Pretty Woman (Orbison), 115
priming, 71–73, *73*
process facilitation skills, 76
process-related mistake, 29
project-based learning, 24, 103, 105, 119, 134

rapport-building techniques, 43–46, *45*
Ratey, J.J., 61, 185
redundancies, 27–29
reflective learners, 87–90
reflective moments, 49
reflective teaching, 33
relative comfort, 2
release mechanism. *See* press and release
risk-taking, 32, 84, 90, 180
Roggenbaum, Frances, 211, 212

routines, 2, 5, 16, 17, 65, 75, 90, 97, 149, 150, 152, 157
Rowe, M., 52
running gags, 36

sage-on-the-stage approach, 33
sarcasm, 38, 43
Sattes, B.D., 75, 76
Schmidt, L., 192, 207, 208
school improvement plan (SIP), 205, 208
Schwab, J., 78
Scozzi, N., 56
self-assessment, 90
self-awareness, 21
self-reflection, 196
Serravallo, J., 159
silence, 16, 49, 51–53, *52*, 71, 76, 134, 149, 178
Silver, D., 192, 195
Simeral, A., 196
simultaneity principle, 72
single cue for bringing students back, 149–52
slavery, 184
slide presentation, 4, 119–22, 126
Smith, D., 32, 92, 146, 189
social media, 13
social skills, 4, 106, 165, 167, 168
Softening the Edges: Assessment Practices That Honor K-12 Teachers and Learners (White), 90
Soltner, Gene, 200
Sommers, W.A., 204, 205
sophomores, 92, 201
speaking skills, 13–14 25, 47, 70, 72, 77, 85, 103, 106, 119, 135, 192
squawking and flapping, 43, 44
standing pairs, 65
status quo, 23, 33, 191, 204
Stiggins, R.J., 88
storytelling, 169–72, *170*
Streamlining the Curriculum (Jacobs and Zmuda), 213

INDEX

student-centered classrooms, 47
student-generated questions, 177
student misbehavior, 43
student self- or peer assessment, 174
student-to-student conversations, 130–31
student-to-student relationships, 2, 165, 179
surface-level learners, 33
Syed, Matthew, 196
syn-naps, 61

task cards, 59, 60
Tate, M.L., 37, 112
teacher-centered classrooms, 5, 185
teacher/student conferences, 88
teacher-to-student relationships, 44, 45, 147, 166, 179, 213
test-driven educational system, 35
thinking, 44, 51, 52, 56, 58, 69, 72, 76, 106, 108, 133, 163, 176, 180, 187, 197; convergent thinking, 105; divergent thinking, 12, 105; positive thinking, 196
Think-Pair-Share (TPS) activity, 188
thoughtful praise, 91–94
Toby, 184
tone of voice, 19
toxic learning environments, 36
traditional classroom setting, 60–61
transferring learned skills to collaborative groups, 103–6
transitional gears, 95–98
tried-and-true reaction, 43
Twenge, J.M., 59
two-minute drill, 165–68

unnecessary decisions avoidance, 99–102
U.S. Constitution's Separation of Powers, 75

verbal cue, 150
verbal directions, 3, 99, 100, 101, 135, 153, 154
Virginia standardized assessments, 170
Visible Learning: The Sequel (Hattie), 180
vision, 80, 209
visuals, 5, 96, 100, 101, 103, 109, 119, 120, 126, 129–32, *132*, 134, 138, 149–51, 156, 159
voice, 13, 16, 19, 48, 49, 56, 95, 96, 125, 133–35, 150, 152, 157, 167, 168, 192; command/credible voice, 48, 96, 97, 129, 167, 168, 187; conversational voices/approachable voice, 96, 167; natural voice, 134, 135; pausing, 134; tone of voice, 19
Vygotsky's concept of the zone of proximal development (ZPD), 7

Wagner, T., 4, 25
Walsh, J.A., 75, 76
Wellman, B., 133, 135
White, J.E., 165
White, Joy, 69
White, K., 90, 175
Whoever Makes the Most Mistakes Wins: The Paradox of Innovation (Farson and Keyes), 24
whole-class debriefing, 56
whole-class discussions, 75–78
Wiliam, Dylan, 206
Willis, J., 61
Wilson, Margaret Berry, 150
Wyatt, R.L., 165

yearbook photographer, 145
YMCA, 199

Zierer, K., 158
Zmuda, A., 213
Zoller, K., 167
zone of proximal development (ZPD), 7
Zwiers, J., 47, 63, 78, 161, 165, 177